The National Directory for the Formation, Ministry, and Life of Permanent Deacons in the United States of America

SECOND EDITION

The National Directory for the Formation, Ministry, and Life of Permanent Deacons in the United States of America

SECOND EDITION

This *National Directory for the Formation, Ministry, and Life of Permanent Deacons in the United States of America* is intended to serve the entire Catholic Church in the United States of America. Its principles, norms, and pastoral applications are directed specifically to the Latin Church. Nonetheless, it may be of assistance as a consistent reference for all Churches *sui iuris* in the United States of America in the preparation of the adaptations necessary to address the particular traditions, pastoral life, and requirements of the *Code of Canons of the Eastern Churches*.

UNITED STATES CONFERENCE
OF CATHOLIC BISHOPS

First Printing, August 2021

ISBN 978-1-60137-604-6

Office of the President

3211 FOURTH STREET NE • WASHINGTON DC 20017-1194 • 202-541-3100 • FAX 202-541-3166

Most Reverend José H. Gomez
Archbishop of Los Angeles
President

DECREE OF PROMULGATION

In June 2019, the members of the United States Conference of Catholic Bishops approved the *National Directory for the Formation, Life and Ministry of Permanent Deacons in the United States*, Second Edition.

This action of the United States Conference of Catholic Bishops, made in accord with canon 236 of the Code of Canon Law and with n. 15 of *Ratio fundamentalis institutionis diaconorum permanentium*, was confirmed *ad quinquennium experimenti gratia* by the Congregation for the Clergy (Prot No. 2020 4233), signed by Beniamino Cardinal Stella, Prefect of the Congregation for the Clergy, and Jorge Carlos Patrón Wong, Secretary for Seminaries, and dated November 13, 2020, to be observed in the formation of Permanent Deacons.

As President of the United States Conference of Catholic Bishops, I hereby decree that the effective date of this Decree of Promulgation will be June 9, 2022, the Feast of St. Ephrem the Syrian, Deacon and Doctor of the Church.

Given at the offices of the United States Conference of Catholic Bishops in the city of Washington, the District of Columbia, on the third of August in the year of our Lord 2021.

Most Reverend José H. Gomez
Archbishop of Los Angeles
President

Reverend Michael J.K. Fuller, S.T.D.
General Secretary

Contents

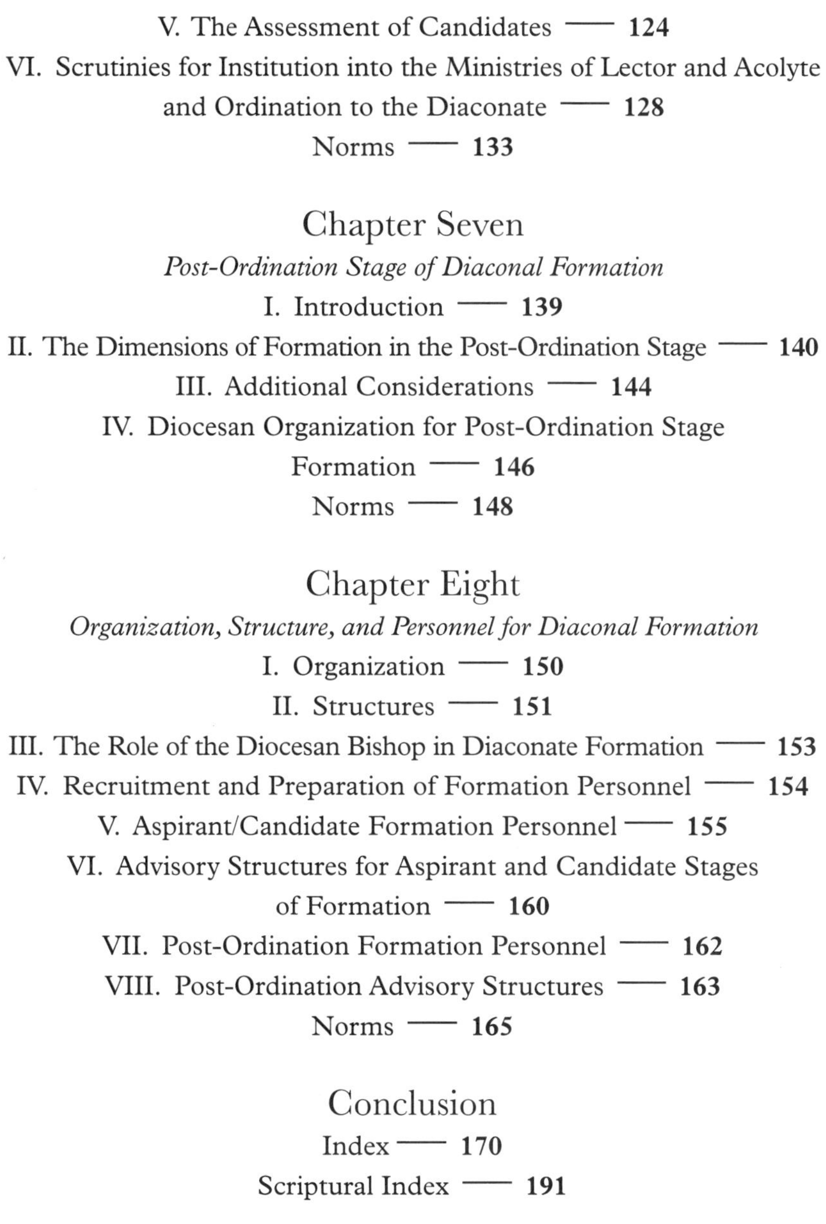

Chapter Seven

Post-Ordination Stage of Diaconal Formation

Chapter Eight

Organization, Structure, and Personnel for Diaconal Formation

Conclusion

Abbreviations

AGD: Second Vatican Council, *Decree on the Missionary Activity of the Church* (*Ad Gentes Divinitus*) (Washington, DC: United States Catholic Conference, 1965)

ADUS: St. John Paul II, *The Heart of the Diaconate: Servants of the Mysteries of Christ and Servants of Your Brothers and Sisters*, Address to Deacons of the United States, Detroit, Michigan (September 19, 1987)

AP: St. Paul VI, Apostolic Letter *Ad Pascendum* (August 15, 1972)

BNFPD: Congregation for Catholic Education, *Basic Norms for the Formation of Permanent Deacons* (*Ratio Fundamentalis Institutionis Diaconorum Permanentium*) (Washington, DC: United States Catholic Conference, 1998)

CCC: *Catechism of the Catholic Church*, 2nd ed. (Washington, DC: United States Conference of Catholic Bishops–Libreria Editrice Vaticana, 2000)

CCLV: Committee on Clergy, Consecrated Life and Vocations, United States Conference of Catholic Bishops

CIC: *Code of Canon Law Latin-English Edition* (*Codex Iuris Canonici*), trans. Canon Law Society of America (Washington, DC: Canon Law Society of America, 1983)

CL: Congregation for Divine Worship and the Discipline of the Sacraments, Circular Letter, *Scrutinies Regarding Suitability of Candidates for Orders*, Prot. No. 589/97 (November 28, 1997), *www.usccb.org/beliefs-and-teachings/vocations/diaconate/upload/CDVDS28Nov1997.pdf*

DMLPD: Congregation for the Clergy, *Directory for the Ministry and Life of Permanent Deacons* (*Directorium Pro Ministerio et Vita Diaconorum*

Permanentium) (Washington, DC: United States Catholic Conference, 1998)

EG: Pope Francis, Apostolic Exhortation *On the Proclamation of the Gospel in Today's World* (*Evangelii Gaudium*) (Washington, DC: USCCB, 2013)

FP: Bishops' Committee on Marriage and Family, NCCB, *A Family Perspective in Church and Society, Tenth Anniversary Edition* (Washington, DC: United States Catholic Conference, 1998)

GDC: Congregation for the Clergy, *General Directory for Catechesis* (Washington, DC: United States Catholic Conference–Libreria Editrice Vaticana, 1998)

GS: Second Vatican Council, *Pastoral Constitution on the Church in the Modern World* (*Gaudium et Spes*) (Washington, DC: United States Catholic Conference, 1965)

LG: Second Vatican Council, *Dogmatic Constitution on the Church* (*Lumen Gentium*) (Washington, DC: United States Catholic Conference, 1964)

NCCB: National Conference of Catholic Bishops (predecessor to the USCCB in the United States of America)

NSD (1996): Bishops' Committee on the Permanent Diaconate, NCCB, *A National Study on the Permanent Diaconate of the Catholic Church in the United States, 1994-1995* (Washington, DC: United States Catholic Conference, 1996)

OE: Second Vatican Council, *Decree on the Catholic Eastern Churches* (*Orientalium Ecclesiarum*). In *Vatican Council II: Vol. 1: The Conciliar and Post Conciliar Documents*, ed. Austin Flannery (Collegeville, MN: Liturgical Press, 1996)

PDG (1984): Bishops' Committee on the Permanent Diaconate,

NCCB, *Permanent Deacons in the United States: Guidelines on Their Formation and Ministry, 1984 Revision* (Washington, DC: United States Catholic Conference, 1985)

PDO: St. John Paul II, *The Permanent Deacon's Ordination*, Address to the Plenary Assembly of the Congregation for the Clergy (November 30, 1995)

PDV: St. John Paul II, Post-Synodal Apostolic Exhortation *I Will Give You Shepherds (Pastores Dabo Vobis)* (Washington, DC: United States Catholic Conference, 1992)

RM: St. John Paul II, Encyclical *On the Permanent Validity of the Church's Missionary Mandate (Redemptoris Missio)* (Washington, DC: United States Catholic Conference, 1990)

SC: Second Vatican Council, *Constitution on the Sacred Liturgy (Sacrosanctum Concilium)*. In *Vatican Council II: Vol. 1: The Conciliar and Post Conciliar Documents*, ed. Austin Flannery (Collegeville, MN: Liturgical Press, 1996)

STVI: Bishops' Committee on the Liturgy and Bishops' Committee on the Permanent Diaconate, NCCB, *The Deacon: Minister of Word and Sacrament, Study Text VI* (Washington, DC: United States Catholic Conference, 1979)

USCCB: United States Conference of Catholic Bishops

Prayer to the Blessed Virgin Mary

Mary,
Teacher of faith, who by your obedience to the Word of God have cooperated in a remarkable way with the work of redemption, make the ministry of deacons effective by teaching them to hear the Word and to proclaim it faithfully.

Mary,
Teacher of charity, who by your total openness to God's call have cooperated in bringing to birth all the Church's faithful, make the ministry and the life of deacons fruitful by teaching them to give themselves totally to the service of the People of God.

Mary,
Teacher of prayer, who through your maternal intercession have supported and helped the Church from her beginnings, make deacons always attentive to the needs of the faithful by teaching them to come to know the value of prayer.

Mary,
Teacher of humility, who by constantly knowing yourself to be the servant of the Lord were filled with the Holy Spirit, make deacons docile instruments in Christ's work of redemption by teaching them the greatness of being the least of all.

Mary,
Teacher of that service which is hidden, who by your everyday and ordinary life filled with love knew how to cooperate with the salvific plan of God in an exemplary fashion, make deacons good and faithful servants by teaching them the joy of serving the Church with an ardent love. Amen.[1]

---

[1] Adapted from DMLPD, p. 70.

Foreword

THROUGHOUT THE LAST DECADE of the twentieth century, the Congregation for Catholic Education and the Congregation for the Clergy devoted considerable attention to the ordained ministries of priest and deacon. After the publication of the *Basic Norms for the Formation of Priests and the Directory on the Ministry and Life of Priests* in 1994, these two Congregations took up the same issues related to the ordained ministry of permanent deacons. In February 1998, they promulgated the *Basic Norms for the Formation of Permanent Deacons* and the *Directory on the Life and Ministry of Permanent Deacons*. In a Joint Declaration and Introduction, the prefects of these two Congregations offered these documents as directives "of which due account is to be taken by the Episcopal Conferences when preparing their respective 'Rationes.' As with the *Ratio fundamentalis institutionis sacerdotalis*, the Congregation offers this aid to the various Episcopates to facilitate them in discharging adequately the prescriptions of canon 236 of the Code of Canon Law and to ensure for the Church, unity, earnestness and completeness in the formation of permanent Deacons."[1]

After years of extensive consultation and preparation, the *National Directory for the Formation, Ministry, and Life of Permanent Deacons in the United States* received the *recognitio* from the Holy See on October 30, 2004. The *National Directory* was then officially promulgated by the president of the United States Conference of Catholic Bishops, on December 26, 2004, the Feast of St. Stephen, Deacon and Martyr. This Second Edition of the *National Directory* went through extensive review and some meaningful revisions. It received *recognitio* from the Holy See on November 13, 2020. The date of official promulgation by the President of the United States Conference of Catholic Bishops is June 9, 2022, the Memorial of St. Ephrem, Deacon, Confessor, and Doctor of the Church.

I would like to remind bishops of the availability of a visit of a consultation team to diocesan permanent diaconate formation programs as a resource offered by the CCLV Committee to assist in strengthening diaconate programs. When a diaconal program is to be introduced or substantially modified, or a program previously on hold is reactivated, the diocesan bishop is welcome to submit a proposal to the CCLV Chairman for its evaluation. The specific elements to be included in the proposal and applied by the committee in its review are available from the CCLV Secretariat.

In the name of the Bishops' Committee on Clergy, Consecrated Life and Vocations, and the United States Conference of Catholic Bishops, I express our gratitude for the participation of all who assisted in the revision of the *National Directory*. Our heartfelt thanks to all those who serve so generously as deacons, as well as their families, pastors, and coworkers in ministry.

Bishop James Checchio, Diocese of Metuchen, New Jersey
Chair, Bishops' Committee on Clergy, Consecrated Life and Vocations

---

[1] Congregation for Catholic Education and Congregation for the Clergy, "Joint Declaration and Introduction," *Basic Norms for the Formation of Permanent Deacons/ Directory for the Ministry and Life of Permanent Deacons* (Vatican City: Libreria Editrice Vaticana, 1998), p. 8.

The National Directory for the Formation, Ministry, and Life of Permanent Deacons in the United States of America

SECOND EDITION

Preface

I.
The Diaconate in the Second Vatican Council and the Post-Conciliar Period: A Historical Overview[1]

1.

ONE OF THE GREAT LEGACIES of the Second Vatican Council was its renewal and encouragement of the Order of Deacons throughout the entire Catholic Church. The Council's decisions on the diaconate flowed out of the bishops' discussions on the sacramental nature of the Church. As noted in the final report of the 1985 extraordinary synod of bishops, the Fathers of the Council present in concise, descriptive, and complementary images a comprehensive magisterial teaching: The Church is "mystery," "sacrament," "communion," and "mission."[2] The Church is "like a sacrament or as a sign and instrument both of a very closely knit union with God and of the unity of the whole human race."[3] "In her whole being and in all her members, the Church is sent to announce, bear witness, make present, and spread the mystery of the communion of the Holy Trinity."[4] This "missionary mandate"[5] is the Church's sacred right and obligation.[6] Through the proclamation of God's Word, in sacramental celebrations, and in response to the needs of others, especially in her ministry of charity, "the Church is Christ's instrument . . . 'the universal sacrament of salvation,' by which Christ is 'at once manifesting and actualizing the mystery of God's love for men.'"[7]

2.

Central to the Second Vatican Council's teaching on the Church is the service or ministry bestowed by Christ upon the Apostles and their successors. The office of bishop "is a true service, which in sacred literature is significantly called '*diakonia*' or ministry."[8] The Council Fathers teach that the bishops, with priests and deacons as helpers, have by divine institution taken the place of the Apostles as pastors of the Church.[9] Priests and deacons are seen as complementary but subordinate participants in the one apostolic ministry bestowed by Christ upon the Apostles, with Peter as their head, and continued through their successors, the bishops, in union with the Roman Pontiff.[10] When discussing Holy Orders as one of the sacraments "at the service of communion" (along with Matrimony), the *Catechism of the Catholic Church* teaches that these two sacraments "are directed towards the salvation of others; if they contribute as well to personal salvation, it is through service to others that they do so. They confer a particular mission in the Church and serve to build up the People of God."[11]

3.

In the *Dogmatic Constitution on the Church*, the *Decree on the Missionary Activity of the Church*, and the *Decree on the Catholic Eastern Churches*, the Second Vatican Council reestablished the diaconate "as a proper and permanent rank of the hierarchy."[12] The Sacred Order of Deacons is to be "a driving force for the Church's service or *diakonia* toward the local Christian communities, and as a sign or sacrament of the Lord Christ himself, who 'came not to be served but to serve.'"[13] "The deacon's ministry of service is linked with the missionary dimension of the Church: the missionary efforts of the deacon will embrace the ministry of word, ministry of liturgy, and works of charity which, in their turn, are carried into daily life. Mission includes witness to Christ in a secular profession or occupation."[14] Further, "neither should the prospect of the mission *ad gentes* be lacking, wherever circumstances require and permit it."[15] In its renewal the Order of Deacons is permanently restored as "a living icon of Christ the Servant within the Church."[16]

4.

Following the closing of the Second Vatican Council, St. Paul VI formally implemented the renewal of the diaconate. In his apostolic letter *Sacrum Diaconatus Ordinem*, he reestablished the Order of Deacons as a permanent ministry in the Catholic Church.[17] The apostolic constitution *Pontificalis Romani Recognitio* promulgated new liturgical rites for the conferral of the Sacrament of Holy Orders upon bishops, priests, and deacons in the Latin Rite.[18] The apostolic letter *Ad Pascendum* established norms concerning the Order of Deacons.[19] The apostolic letter *Ministeria Quaedam* addressed the suppression in the Latin Rite of first tonsure, the minor orders, and the subdiaconate; established norms for entrance into the clerical state; and instituted the stable ministries of lector and acolyte.[20]

II.
The Diaconate in the United States of America

5.

Since the Second Vatican Council consigned the decision of the restoration of the diaconate to individual episcopal conferences, the bishops of the United States of America voted in the spring of 1968 to petition the Holy See for authorization. In their letter of May 2, 1968, the bishops presented the following reasons for the request:

a. To complete the hierarchy of sacred orders and to enrich and strengthen the many and various diaconal ministries at work in the United States of America with the sacramental grace of the diaconate
b. To enlist a new group of devout and competent men in the active ministry of the Church
c. To aid in extending needed liturgical and charitable services to the faithful in both large urban and small rural communities
d. To provide an official and sacramental presence of the Church in areas of secular life, as well as in communities within large cities and sparsely settled regions where few or no priests are available
e. To provide an impetus and source for creative adaptations of diaconal ministries to the rapidly changing needs of our society

6.

On August 30, 1968, the Apostolic Delegate informed the United States of America bishops that St. Paul VI had agreed to their request. In November of that year, a standing committee on the diaconate was created by the National Conference of Catholic Bishops (NCCB). In 1971, the conference approved and authorized the publication of the committee's document titled *Permanent Deacons in the United States: Guidelines on Their Formation and Ministry*.[21] These *Guidelines* served the Church in the United States of America well as it began to assimilate the new ministry of deacons.[22] In February 1977, the committee organized a comprehensive study "to assess the extent to which the vision" for the diaconate had been realized.[23] The results of that appraisal were published in 1981 under the title *A National Study of the Permanent Diaconate in the United States*.[24] The report acknowledged that the purpose of the diaconate and its integration into the life of the Church in the United States of America had not yet been fully realized. Building on that *Study*, the NCCB commissioned the revision of the 1971 *Guidelines*. In November 1984, new guidelines were published under the title *Permanent Deacons in the United States: Guidelines on Their Formation and Ministry, 1984 Revision*.[25]

7.

The committee approved and authorized the publication of a series of monographs as part of a structured national catechesis on the diaconate. In collaboration with the committee, the Bishops' Committee on the Liturgy issued the document *The Deacon: Minister of Word and Sacrament, Study Text VI* (1979), which was devoted to the liturgical ministries of the deacon.[26] A second monograph addressed *The Service Ministry of the Deacon* (1988),[27] and a third monograph, *Foundations for the Renewal of the Diaconate* (1993), offered an international and historical perspective on the theology of the diaconate.[28] In 1998, the committee sponsored the production of a video, *Deacons: Ministers of Justice and Charity*, which highlighted some of the diverse service ministries of deacons in the United States of America.[29]

III.
Subsequent Developments

8.

The documents of the Second Vatican Council convey "a great deal about bishops and laity and very little about priests and deacons."[30] In 1990, St. John Paul II convened an Extraordinary Synod of Bishops to consider the life and ministry of priests within the Church in order "to close this gap on behalf of priests with the completion of some important initiatives . . . for example . . . the publication of the post-synodal Apostolic Exhortation *Pastores Dabo Vobis*[31] and, as an implementation of this document, the *Directory on the Ministry and Life of Priests*.[32]"[33]

9.

Seeking further to promote "a certain unity of direction and clarification of concepts, as well as . . . practical encouragement and more clearly defined pastoral objectives,"[34] the Congregation for the Clergy and the Congregation for Catholic Education organized a plenary assembly to study the diaconate. This gathering responded to concerns that had surfaced through the *ad limina* visits and reports of the bishops since the restoration of the diaconate had begun.[35] The members of the congregations and their consultants convened in November 1995. St. John Paul II met with the participants and focused his comments on the identity, mission, and ministry of the deacon in the Church.[36]

10.

Following this plenary assembly, the Congregation for the Clergy published a *Directory for the Ministry and Life of Permanent Deacons;* and concurrently the Congregation for Catholic Education issued *Basic Norms for the Formation of Permanent Deacons*. Both documents provide episcopal conferences with directives and norms on the selection, formation, and pastoral care of aspirants, candidates, and deacons in accord with the intent of the Second Vatican Council and the subsequent teachings of St. Paul VI and St. John Paul II.[37] These documents were promulgated as a joint text by St. John Paul II on February 22, 1998, the Feast of the Chair of Peter.[38]

11.

Between 1995 and 1996, the NCCB's Bishops' Committee on the Diaconate, under the chairmanship of Most Rev. Dale J. Melczek, issued three documents: (1) *Protocol for the Incardination/Excardination of Deacons*, (2) *Policy Statement: Self-Study Instrument and Consultation*

Team Procedures,[39] and (3) *A National Study on the Permanent Diaconate in the Catholic Church in the United States, 1994-1995, published in 1996*.[40] The 1996 *Study* focused on concerns that had surfaced at a special assembly of the NCCB that was convened to address vocations and future church leadership. Those concerns included the identity of the deacon, his effective incorporation into the pastoral ministries of dioceses and parishes, and the need for better screening and training.[41] The 1996 *Study* confirmed the success of the restoration of the diaconate in the United States of America in terms of the number of vocations and in its significant, almost indispensable service to parochial communities. However, the *Study* also substantiated the concerns raised by the bishops and provided guidance in addressing them.[42]

12.

In 1994, the committee organized a national conference for deacons. Its purpose was to celebrate the twenty-fifth anniversary of their restoration in the Church in the United States of America. The first National Catholic Diaconate Conference was convened in the Archdiocese of New Orleans. The theme of this conference was "*Diaconate: A Great and Visible Sign of the Work of the Holy Spirit*." In June 1997, participants gathered in the Archdiocese of Milwaukee and there explored the theme "*The Deacon in a Diaconal Church: Minister of Justice and Charity*." A third conference was convened in June 2000 in the Diocese of Oakland; the theme of this Jubilee Year 2000 conference was "*The Deacon in the Third Millennium—New Evangelization*."[43] A conference was convened in July 2018 in the Archdiocese of New Orleans to celebrate the fiftieth anniversary of the restoration of the permanent diaconate in the United States. The theme of this conference was "Christ the Servant: Yesterday, Today, Forever."

IV.
The Development of This National Directory

13.

In March 1997, Most Rev. Edward U. Kmiec, chairman of the Bishops' Committee on the Diaconate,[44] convened two subcommittees to oversee the revision of the 1984 *Guidelines*. He named Most Rev. Howard J. Hubbard, DD, and Most Rev. William E. Lori, STD, members of the committee, as co-chairmen for the revision. He appointed Rev. Msgr. Theodore W. Kraus, PhD, past president of the National Association of Diaconate Directors, to serve as the project director. The members of both subcommittees brought varied professional and personal experience to the work and were representative of the geographic, cultural, and social profile of the Church in the United States of America.[45] Their work was assisted by Rev. Kevin Irwin, STD, theological consultant to the committee; Rev. Msgr. William A. Varvaro, STL, JCD, canonical consultant; and Deacon John Pistone, then Executive Director of the Secretariat for the Diaconate, NCCB. In November 1998, Most Rev. Gerald F. Kicanas, STL, PhD, was elected by the conference as chairman of the committee. He invited Cardinal Adam Maida, JCL, JD, STL, and Most Rev. Donald W. Wuerl, STD, to assist the committee as episcopal consultants in furthering the development of the document. Extensive consultation with the bishops and the major superiors of men religious, as well as diocesan directors of the diaconate and the executives of national diaconate organizations, preceded the approval of the document by the NCCB at its general meeting in June 2000. In November 2001, Most Rev. Robert C. Morlino, STD, was elected by the conference as chairman of the committee. Under his chairmanship, the committee revised the document in response to the observations received in March 2002 from the Congregation for Catholic Education and the Congregation for the Clergy. The document was then approved by the USCCB at its general meeting in June 2003.

14.

In January 2013, the USCCB's Committee on Clergy, Consecrated Life, and Vocations (CCLV), under the chairmanship of the Most Rev. Robert Carlson, asked the Committee on Canonical Affairs and Church Governance and the National Association of Diaconate Directors to review the first edition of the *National Directory* and give recommendations for changes to the text. Following its review of these recommendations, CCLV consulted with the body of bishops, who discussed the *National Directory* at their November 2013 regional meetings. Following this consultation, CCLV recommended that the USCCB seek a simple *recognitio* from the Congregation for Clergy to renew the first edition of the *National Directory* for another five years. At the June 2014 plenary assembly, the body of bishops voted unanimously to accept CCLV's recommendation and sought a simple renewal of the *recognitio*. The *recognitio* was received from the Congregation for Clergy in December 2014, with the understanding that the USCCB would update the *National Directory* within five years. In March 2015, Most Rev. Michael F. Burbidge, CCLV Chairman, convened a working group to oversee the revision of the *National Directory*. He named Most Rev. Samuel J. Aquila, member of the committee, as chairman of a working group comprising bishops and experts in the field of the diaconate.[46] In November of 2016 Joseph Cardinal Tobin became CCLV Chairman following his 2015 election. The working group completed a draft of the document in spring 2017, which was then reviewed by the following USCCB Committees: Canonical Affairs and Church Governance, Child and Youth Protection, Cultural Diversity in the Church, Divine Worship, and Doctrine. After revising the document based on the input of the collaborating committees, in September 2017 the CCLV Committee approved a draft of the *National Directory*, 2nd edition, and, in accord with the *Regulations Regarding United States Conference of Catholic Bishops Statements and Publications*, submitted it for review to the Committee on Canonical Affairs and Church Governance (CACG) and the Committee on Doctrine. In June 2018, having revised the draft document based on the recommendations of the Doctrine and CACG Committees, the CCLV Committee approved the *National Directory for the Formation, Ministry, and Life of Permanent Deacons in the United States*, 2nd edition, and recommended that the draft be presented to the body of bishops in the General Assembly session in November 2018 following the required authorization of the Administrative Committee if the agenda would allow. Given the extraordinary circumstances of the Church in the United States in the fall of 2018, the Administrative Committee decided to postpone the discussion and vote. In 2019 the CCLV Committee requested that the Administrative Committee approve the inclusion of the *National Directory* on the June 2019 General Assembly agenda for discussion and vote. The United States Conference of Catholic Bishops approved the document at the General

Assembly meeting in June 2019. Later that summer it was submitted to the Congregation for the Clergy for *recognitio*. In November of 2019 Most Rev. James Checchio became CCLV chairman following his 2018 election. Under his chairmanship the CCLV Committee revised the document based on recommendations received from the Congregation for the Clergy in 2020. The Congregation for the Clergy granted the *recognitio* of the *National Directory*, 2nd edition, in November of 2020.

V.
The Objective and Interpretation of This *National Directory*

15.

This *National Directory* is prescribed for the use of the diocesan bishop, as well as those responsible for its implementation. The specifications prescribed in this *National Directory* are to be incorporated by each diocese of the conference when preparing or updating its respective diaconal formation program and when formulating policies for the ministry and life of its deacons.[47] At the same time, diocesan bishops may make pastoral accommodations in the recruitment, education, and ongoing formation of permanent deacons, particularly those from, or called to serve, underserved ethnic or cultural communities.[48]

16.

This *National Directory* is normative throughout the dioceses of the USCCB as well as within the Personal Ordinariate of the Chair of St. Peter. Reflecting fifty years of experience with the reestablished diaconate in the United States of America, this *National Directory* will guide and harmonize the formation programs drawn up by each diocese of the conference, which "at times vary greatly from one to another."[49]

17.

When a diaconal formation program is introduced or substantially modified, or a program previously on hold is reactivated, the diocesan bishop is encouraged to submit a proposal to CCLV for its evaluation. The specific elements to be included in the proposal and applied by the committee in its review are available from the CCLV's secretariat.

18.

Finally, this document adopts as its own the concluding directive of the Congregation for Catholic Education: May the ordinaries, "to whom the present document is given, ensure that it becomes an object of attentive reflection in communion with their priests and communities. It will be an important point of reference for those Churches in which the permanent diaconate is a living and active reality; for the others, it will be an effective invitation to appreciate the value of that precious gift of the Spirit which is diaconal service."[50]

19.

Gratefully conscious of those who have served on CCLV, the USCCB acknowledges the direction of Most Rev. Michael F. Burbidge, under whose chairmanship the present effort was begun, His Eminence Cardinal Joseph Tobin, CSsR, under whose chairmanship the document's revisions were composed and approved by the bishops, and Most Rev. James Checchio under whose chairmanship it has been brought to conclusion.

---

[1] There is one Sacred Order of Deacons. Some deacons, who are in transition to ordination to the priesthood, usually exercise the Order of Deacons for a brief period of time. The vast majority of deacons live and exercise it, however, as a permanent rank of the hierarchy in both the Latin and Eastern Catholic Churches *sui iuris*. This *Directory* addresses only the formation, ministry, and life of permanent deacons in the Latin Church.

In 1995, as authorized by the General Secretary of the NCCB, the word "permanent" was discontinued in the title of the bishops' committee, in the NCCB' Secretariat for the Diaconate, and in its communiqués. In this text, therefore, the word "permanent" is not used unless it is contained in a specific quotation or in the title or committee of a publication. When the word "diaconate" is mentioned in this text, it refers to those who seek to be or are ordained permanent deacons.

In 2001, the NCCB, the "canonical entity," and the United States Catholic Conference, the "civil entity," were canonically and civilly reconstituted as the United States Conference of Catholic Bishops, or USCCB. This reconstituted entity is implied in this document except in those circumstances where the text requires reference to the previous nomenclatures.

[2] Extraordinary Synod of Bishops, Final Report *Ecclesia Sub Verbo Dei Mysteria Christi Celebrans Pro Salute Mundi* (December 7, 1995).

[3] LG, no. 1.

[4] CCC, no. 738.

[5] CCC, no. 849.

[6] AGD, nos. 15-16.

[7] CCC, no. 776. See LG, nos. 9-17, 48; GS, nos. 1-3, 26-30, 32, 45.

[8] LG, no. 24. See Acts 1:17, 25; Acts 21:19; Rom 11:13; 1 Tm 1:12; St. John Paul II, Post-Synodal Apostolic Exhortation *The Vocation and the Mission of the Lay Faithful in the Church and in the World (Christifideles Laici)* (Washington, DC: United States Catholic Conference, December 30, 1988), no. 22.

[9] LG, nos. 18, 20.

[10] LG, nos. 20. See nos. 22-23.

[11] CCC, no. 1534.

[12] LG, no. 29. See AGD, nos. 15-16; OE, no. 17.

[13] AP, citing Mt 20:28.

[14] DMLPD, no. 27.

[15] BNFPD, no. 88.

[16] BNFPD, no. 11.

[17] St. Paul VI, Apostolic Letter Motu Proprio *Sacrum Diaconatus Ordinem* (June 18, 1967), *www.vatican.va/content/paul-vi/en/motu_proprio/documents/hf_p-vi_motu-proprio_19670618_sacrum-diaconatus.html.*

[18] St. Paul VI, Apostolic Constitution *Pontificalis Romani Recognitio* (June 18, 1968), *www.vatican.va/content/paul-vi/la/apost_constitutions/documents/hf_p-vi_apc_19680618_pontificalis-romani.html (Latin only).*

[19] AP.

[20] St. Paul VI, Apostolic *Letter Ministeria Quaedam* (August 15, 1972), *www.vatican.va/content/paul-vi/la/motu_proprio/documents/hf_p-vi_motu-proprio_19720815_ministeria-quaedam.html* (Latin only).

[21] Bishops' Committee on the Permanent Diaconate, NCCB, *Permanent Deacons in the United States: Guidelines on Their Formation and Ministry* (Washington, DC: United States Catholic Conference, 1971). The committee, under its first chairman, Most Rev. Ernest L. Unterkoefler, prepared the original 1971 edition of these *guidelines.*

[22] The diaconate has grown remarkably in the United States. According to statistics of the USCCB Secretariat for the Diaconate, there were, in 1971, 58 deacons and 529 candidates and, in 1975, 1,074 deacons and 2,243 candidates. By 1980, the number of deacons had quadrupled to 4,656, with 2,514 candidates. By December 31, 2001, more than 14,000 deacons were serving in the dioceses of the United States and territorial sees. According to the Center for Applied Research in the Apostolate (CARA), as of 2015 "it can be estimated that there are 18,558 permanent deacons in the United States today." Of this number, "it can be estimated that there are 14,588 deacons active in ministry in the United States today, or about 79 percent of all permanent deacons." Mary L. Gautier and Thomas P. Gaunt, *A Portrait of the Permanent Diaconate: A Study for the U.S. Conference of Catholic Bishops 2014-2015* (Washington, DC: CARA/Georgetown University, May 2015).

[23] Bishops' Committee on the Permanent Diaconate, NCCB, *A National Study of the Permanent Diaconate in the United States* (Washington, DC: United States Catholic Conference, 1981), 1.

[24] Bishops' Committee on the Permanent Diaconate, *National Study*, 1.

[25] PDG (1984). The committee under the chairmanship of Most Rev. John J. Snyder began the revision. It was completed under the chairmanship of Most Rev. John F. Kinney.

[26] STVI.

[27] Bishops' Committee on the Permanent Diaconate, NCCB, *Service Ministry of the Deacon*, written by Rev. Timothy J. Shugrue (Washington, DC: United States Catholic Conference, 1988).

[28] Bishops' Committee on the Permanent Diaconate, NCCB, Foundations for the Renewal of the Diaconate (Washington, DC: United States Catholic Conference, 1993).

[29] Bishops' Committee on the Diaconate, NCCB, Deacons: Ministers of Justice and Charity [video], ed. Deacon Richard Folger (1998).

[30] Most Rev. Crescenzio Sepe, Secretary of the Congregation for the Clergy, Address to the National Catholic Diaconate Conference, New Orleans, LA (July 21, 1994).

[31] PDV.

[32] Congregation for the Clergy, *Directory on the Ministry and Life of Priests* (Washington, DC: Libreria Editrice Vaticana–United States Catholic Conference, 1994).

[33] Sepe, Address.

[34] BNFPD and DMLPD, joint declaration.

[35] These concerns centered upon an incorrect understanding of the role of the deacon in the hierarchical structure of the Church, of the doctrine on ministries, on the role of the laity and the role of women, as well as on concerns regarding selection, adequate intellectual formation, and proper pastoral ministries for deacons. See Sepe, Address.

[36] PDO.

[37] BNFPD and DMLPD, joint introduction, no. 2; see BNFPD, no. 14.

[38] BNFPD, no. 90; DMLPD, no. 82. Additional Vatican documents relevant to the formation and ministry of deacons include the following:

1. *Guide for Catechists* (1993), issued by the Congregation for Evangelization of Peoples, which proposes educational and formational models. As required by the Congregation for Catholic Education in BNFPD, diaconal formation is to encompass more than catechist formation and is to be more analogous to the formation of priests. *Guide for Catechists* provides universal guidelines for catechist formation.

2. The *General Directory for Catechesis* (1997), from the Congregation for the Clergy, provides insightful criteria in proposing appropriate adult education methodologies and for establishing parameters for an authentic and complete theological study. *The Instruction on Certain Questions Regarding the Collaboration of the Non-Ordained Faithful in the Sacred Ministry of Priest* (1997), signed by the heads of eight dicasteries of the

Holy See, offers explanations on the appropriate collaboration between the ordained ministers of the Church and the non-ordained faithful.

3. In 1997, the Congregation for Divine Worship and the Discipline of the Sacraments issued a Circular Letter (cited herein as CL) to diocesan bishops and religious ordinaries establishing criteria regarding the suitability of candidates to be admitted to sacred orders and further directing the establishment of a diocesan board to oversee the scrutinies of candidates before the reception of the rite of candidacy, the ministry of lector, the ministry of acolyte, and ordination to the diaconate and priesthood. This document is essential in the formulation of admission and selection policies for diaconal candidates.

4. The Pontifical Council for Promoting Christian Unity issued a supplementary document to its *Directory for the Application of Principles and Norms on Ecumenism* (1993), namely, the *Ecumenical Dimension in the Formation of Those Engaged in Pastoral Work* (1997). This document specifies that an ecumenical dimension is to be included in diaconal formation and ministry.

5. The encyclical letter *On the Relationship Between Faith and Reason (Fides et Ratio)* (1998), issued by St. John Paul II, establishes academic parameters to be included in the intellectual and human dimensions of diaconal formation.

6. The post-synodal apostolic exhortation *The Church in America (Ecclesia in America)* (1999), issued by St. John Paul II, addresses the new evangelization in the Church in America and makes reference to the role of the deacon in that ministry.

Additional documents of relevance that were released subsequent to the first edition of this *National Directory* include the following: Congregation for Divine Worship and the Discipline of the Sacraments, Instruction *Redemptionis Sacramentum* (2004); Pope Benedict XVI, Apostolic Letter Motu Proprio *Omnium in Mentem* (2009); and Congregation for the Doctrine of the Faith, *Normae de Gravioribus Delictis* (2012).

[39] Bishops' Committee on the Diaconate, NCCB, *Protocol for the Incardination/ Excardination of Deacons* (1995); and Bishops' Committee on the Diaconate, NCCB, *Policy Statement: Self-Study Instrument and Consultation Team Procedures* (1995).

[40] NSD (1996).

[41] Cardinal Joseph Bernardin, "Summary Comments on the Permanent Diaconate," Special Assembly of the NCCB, St. John's Abbey, Collegeville, MN (June 9-16, 1986), in *Vocations and Future Church Leadership* (Washington, DC: United States Catholic Conference, 1986).

[42] NSD (1996), 13-16.

[43] In 1994 Most Rev. Crescenzio Sepe, DD, Secretary of the Congregation for the Clergy, addressed the National Catholic Diaconate Conference on the background and preparations being made for the plenary assembly scheduled for November 1995. In 1997, Cardinal Darío Castrillón Hoyos, Pro-Prefect of the Congregation for the Clergy, spoke on "The Deacon in the Life and Mission of the Church," providing insight on the *Directory* being prepared by the Congregation. In 2000, Most Rev. Gabriel Montalvo, Apostolic Nuncio to the United States, addressed the role of the deacon in the Church's mission of new evangelization.

[44] See note 1 in this preface regarding the removal of the word "permanent" from title of the Bishops' Committee on the Diaconate.

[45] The members of the Subcommittee on Formation and Curriculum included the following: Most Rev. Howard Hubbard, Bishop of Albany (chairman); for **Deacon Ministry and Life**, Deacon James Swiler, Director of Diaconate Formation, Archdiocese of New Orleans (facilitator); Mrs. Bonnie Swiler, Archdiocese of New Orleans; Sr. Yvonne Lerner, OSB, Director of Diaconate Formation, Diocese of Little Rock; for **Formation**, Dr. Ann Healey, Director of Deacon Formation, Diocese of Fort Worth (facilitator); Rev. Michael Galvan, Pastor, St. Joseph Church, Pinole, CA; Deacon James Keeley, Director of Diaconate Formation, Diocese of San Diego; Mrs. Jeanne Schrempf, Director of Religious Education, Diocese of Albany; Deacon Enrique Alonso, President, National Association of Hispanic Deacons; for **Diocesan Structures and Selection**, Mr. Timothy C. Charek, Director, Deacon Formation Program, Archdiocese of Milwaukee (facilitator); Most Rev. Dominic Carmon, SVD, Auxiliary Bishop of the Archdiocese of New Orleans, member of the Bishops' Committee on the Diaconate; Rev. Richard W. Woy, Vicar for Clergy, Archdiocese of Baltimore; for **Curriculum**, Deacon Stephen Graff, Dean of Students, St. Bernard's Institute, Rochester, NY (facilitator); Rev. Msgr. Ernest J. Fiedler, Rector, Cathedral of the Immaculate Conception, Diocese of Kansas City–St. Joseph, and former Executive Director, NCCB Secretariat for the Diaconate; Rev. Bryan Massingale, Vice Rector, St. Francis Seminary, Milwaukee, WI; Rev. Alejandro Castillo, SVD, Director of the Office for Hispanic Affairs, California Catholic Conference, Sacramento, CA; Rev. Robert Egan, SJ, St. Michael's Institute, Spokane, WA; Mr. Neal Parent, Executive Director, National Conference of Catechetical Leadership, Washington, DC; Dr. Seung Ai Yang, Professor of Scripture, The Jesuit School of Theology, Berkeley, CA.

The members of the Subcommittee for Theological and Canonical Revision included Most Rev. William Lori, Auxiliary Bishop of Washington, DC (chairman); for **Theology**, Rev. Msgr. Paul Langsfeld, Vice Rector, St. Mary's Seminary, Emmitsburg, MD (facilitator); Deacon Samuel M. Taub, Diocese of Arlington, former Executive Director, NCCB Secretariat for the Diaconate; Sr. Patricia Simpson, OP, Prioress, Dominican Sisters of San Rafael, CA, and former Director of Diaconate Formation, Diocese of Sacramento; Rev. Frank Silva, Pastor, Immaculate Conception Church, Malden, MA, and former Director of Diaconate, Archdiocese of Boston; for **Spirituality**, Deacon William T. Ditewig, Director of Pastoral Services and Ministry Formation, Diocese of Davenport (facilitator); Mrs. Diann Ditewig, Davenport, IA; Most Rev. Allen H. Vigneron, Auxiliary Bishop of the Archdiocese of Detroit, and Rector, Sacred Heart Major Seminary, Detroit, MI; Deacon James Condill, President, National Association of Deacon Organizations; for Ministry, Rev. Msgr. Timothy Shugrue, Pastor, Immaculate Conception Church, Montclair, NJ, and former Director of Diaconate, Archdiocese of Newark (facilitator); Rev. Edward Salmon, Vicar, Diaconate Community, Archdiocese of Chicago; Rev. Msgr. Joseph Roth, President, National Association of Diaconate Directors; Deacon John Stewart, President, National Association of African-American Catholic Deacons.

Rev. Msgr. Theodore W. Kraus, Director of Diaconate, Diocese of Oakland, the *Directory*'s project director, served *ex officio* on each subcommittee and working unit.

[46] The members of CCLV from 2013 to 2016 were Bishop Michael Burbidge (chairman), Archbishop Samuel Aquila, Bishop Earl Boyea, Bishop William Callahan,

OFM Conv, Bishop Arturo Cepeda, Bishop Thomas Daly, Bishop Curtis Guillory, Bishop John Noonan, and Bishop Daniel Thomas. Consultants to CCLV from 2013 to 2016 were Msgr. Richard Henning, Msgr. Christopher Schreck, Sr. Rose McDermott, SSJ, Deacon Gerald DuPont, and Mrs. Rosemary Sullivan.

The members of CCLV from 2016 to 2019 were Cardinal Joseph W. Tobin, CSsR (chairman), Archbishop Samuel Aquila, Archbishop Charles Thompson, Archbishop John Wester, Bishop Earl Boyea, Bishop Arturo Cepeda, Bishop James Checchio, Bishop Thomas Daly, and Bishop Michael Olson. Consultants to CCLV from 2016 to 2019 were Msgr. Roberto Garza, Fr. Cletus Kiley, Deacon Raphael Duplechain, Sr. Sharon Euart, RSM, and Mrs. Rosemary Sullivan. Members of the *National Directory*, Second Edition, working group were Archbishop Samuel Aquila (chairman), Archbishop Alexander K. Sample, Bishop Michael Sis, Bishop Alberto Rojas, Fr. Shawn McKnight, Deacon Justin Green, Deacon Gerald DuPont, Deacon James Keating, and Msgr. Christopher Schreck (writer). Contributing as well were the National Association of Diaconate Directors (Deacon Thomas Dubois, Executive Director) and the Catholic Association of Teachers of Homiletics (Dr. Susan McGurgan, President).

Members of the CCLV Committee from 2019-2020 were Bishop James Checchio (Chairman), Archbishop Samuel Aquila, Archbishop Charles Thompson, Bishop Juan Miguel Betancourt, Bishop Earl Boyea, Bishop Ronald Hicks, Bishop David Malloy, and Bishop Daniel Mueggenborg. Consultants to the CCLV Committee from 2019-2020 were Sr. Sharon Euart, RSM, Rev. Timothy Kesicki, SJ, Rev. Msgr. Todd Lajiness, and Mrs. Rosemary Sullivan.

[47] BNFPD and DMLPD, joint declaration; see BNFPD, nos. 14, 17.

[48] "Hispanics account for 71 percent of the growth of the Catholic population in the United States since 1960. Approximately 60 percent of all Catholics younger than 18 are Hispanic. The fastest-growing group in the church in this country is Asian Catholics. Hundreds of thousands of Catholics from Africa and the Caribbean have made the U.S. their home." Hosffman Ospino, "Keynote at Convocation of Catholic Leaders," July 2, 2017, in *Origins* 47:11: 164.

[49] BNFPD, nos. 2, 14.

[50] BNFPD, no. 90.

Chapter One

Doctrinal Understanding of the Diaconate

I.
Introduction

20.

THIS *NATIONAL DIRECTORY* offers some theological points of reference based upon relevant magisterial teaching. As the Congregation for Catholic Education explains, "The almost total disappearance of the permanent diaconate from the Church of the West for more than a millennium has certainly made it more difficult to understand the profound reality of this ministry. However, it cannot be said for that reason that the theology of the diaconate has no authoritative points of reference. . . . [T]hey are very clear, even if they need to be developed and deepened."[1]

II.
The Sacramental Nature of the Church

21.

Lumen Gentium, the *Dogmatic Constitution on the Church* from the Second Vatican Council, speaks of the Church as "mystery," "sacrament," "communion," and "mission": "The Church is in Christ like a sacrament or as a sign and instrument both of a very closely knit union with God and of the unity of the whole human race."[2] The Church is the People of God, the Body of Christ, and the Temple of the Holy Spirit.[3] It is "the community of faith, hope, and charity" as well as "an entity with visible delineation."[4] "But, the society [formed] with hierarchical [structures] and the Mystical Body of Christ . . . [are] not to be considered as two realities, nor are the visible assembly and the spiritual community, nor the earthly Church and the Church enriched with heavenly things; rather they form one complex reality, which coalesces from a divine and a human element."[5]

22.

Jesus Christ, through his ministry, life, Death, and Resurrection, established in human society and history a new and distinct reality, a community of men and women, through whom "He communicated truth and grace to all."[6] Through the Church, the Good News of Jesus Christ continues to be told and applied to the changing circumstances and challenges of human life. As Christians live their lives in the power of the Holy Spirit and in the assurance of Christ's return in glory, they offer to others a hope to live by, encouraging them also to embrace Christ and overcome the forces of evil. In the sacraments, which symbolize and make real again the gifts of God that are the origin, center, and goal of the Church's life, the power of Jesus Christ's redemption is again and again at work in the world. In her ministry, the Church "encompasses with love all who are afflicted with human suffering and in the poor and afflicted sees the image of her poor and suffering founder. It does all it can to relieve their need and in them it strives to serve Christ."[7] Thus, in the communion of life, love, and service realized under the leadership of the successors of the Apostles, a vision of reconciled humanity is offered to the world.

III.
Ecclesial Communion and Mission

The Sacraments of Christian Initiation: Baptism, Confirmation, and Eucharist

23.

Initiation into the Church, the Body of Christ, comes about first through the Sacrament of Baptism—the outpouring of the Holy Spirit. In Baptism, every member of the Church receives new life in the Spirit and becomes a member of Christ's Body—a participant in the new creation. This new life is strengthened in the Sacrament of Confirmation, through which the baptized receives the Spirit, is more perfectly bound to the Church, and is obliged to bear witness to Christ and to spread and defend the faith by word and deed. In the Sacrament of the Eucharist, the child of God receives the food of new life, the Body and Blood of Christ. In this Holy Communion, Christ unites each of the baptized to all the faithful in one body—the Church: "Baptism, Confirmation, and Eucharist are sacraments of Christian initiation. They ground the common vocation of all Christ's disciples, a vocation to holiness and to the mission of evangelizing the world. They confer the graces needed for the life according to the Spirit during this life as pilgrims on the march towards the homeland."[8] "Communion and mission are profoundly connected with each other, they interpenetrate and mutually imply each other, to the point that communion represents both the source and the fruit of mission: communion gives rise to mission and mission is accomplished in communion. It is always the one and the same Spirit who calls together and unifies the Church and sends her to preach the Gospel 'to the ends of the earth.'"[9]

The Sacrament of Holy Orders

24.

The Church, itself the great sacrament of Christ's presence, rejoices in another "outpouring of the Spirit"[10]—the Sacrament of Holy Orders. Out of the body of initiated believers—anointed in the Holy Spirit through the Sacrament of Baptism, strengthened in the Sacrament of Confirmation, and nurtured with the Bread of Life—Christ calls some to ordained service. The Church, discerning their vocational charism, asks the diocesan bishop to ordain them to *diakonia*.

25.

"Holy Orders is the sacrament through which the mission entrusted by Christ to his apostles [and their successors] continues to be exercised in the Church until the end of time."[11] Thus, it is the sacrament of apostolic ministry: "The mission of the Apostles, which the Lord Jesus continues to entrust to the Pastors of his people, is a true service, significantly referred to in Sacred Scripture as 'diakonia,' namely, service or ministry."[12] This *diakonia* "is exercised on different levels by those who from antiquity have been called bishops, priests and deacons."[13] "The ordained ministries, apart from the persons who receive them, are a grace for the entire Church."[14] "These two terms—apostle and servant—go together. They can never be separated. They are like the two sides of a medal. Those who proclaim Jesus are called to serve, and those who serve proclaim Jesus."[15]

26.

The *Catechism of the Catholic Church* speaks of the Sacrament of Holy Orders in this way:

> Catholic doctrine, expressed in the liturgy, the Magisterium, and the constant practice of the Church, recognizes that there are two degrees of ministerial participation in the priesthood of Christ: the episcopacy and the presbyterate. The diaconate is intended to help and serve them. For this reason the term *sacerdos* in current usage denotes bishops and priests but not deacons. Yet Catholic doctrine teaches that the degrees of priestly participation (episcopate and presbyterate) and the degree of service (diaconate) are all three conferred by a sacramental act called "ordination," that is, by the Sacrament of Holy Orders.[16]

27.

St. Paul points out that the Holy Spirit is the source of all ministries in the Church and that these services are quite distinct (see 1 Cor 12:4-11; Rom 12:4-8). The distribution of ministerial gifts follows a design set by Christ: "In the building up of Christ's Body various members and functions have their part to play. There is only one Spirit who, according to His own richness and the needs of the ministries, gives His different gifts for the welfare of the Church. What has a special place among these gifts is the grace of the apostles to whose authority the Spirit Himself subjected even those who are endowed with charisms."[17]

IV.
The Reestablished Order of Deacons

28.

The Fathers of the Second Vatican Council, taking seriously the role of the deacon to which St. Paul refers in his First Letter to Timothy, remind us that "those who serve well as deacons gain good standing and much confidence in their faith in Christ Jesus" (3:13). It was for serious pastoral and theological reasons that the Council decided to reestablish the Order of Deacons as a permanent rank in the hierarchy of the Church.

29.

The Sacrament of Holy Orders marks deacons "with an *imprint* ('character') which cannot be removed and which configures them to Christ, who made himself the 'deacon' or servant of all."18 For this level of Holy Orders, Christ the Servant calls, and the Church asks the bishop to ordain, deacons to be consecrated witnesses to service. In his post-synodal exhortation *The Church in America*, St. John Paul II makes his own the words of the bishops of that gathering: "We see with joy how deacons 'sustained by the grace of the Sacrament, in the ministry (*diakonia*) of the liturgy, of the word and of charity are at the service of the People of God, in communion with the Bishop and his priests.'"19

30.

Ordination confers an outpouring of the Holy Spirit. It configures the deacon to Christ's consecration and mission. It constitutes the deacon as a sacred minister by the Sacrament of Holy Orders. He is "consecrated and deputed to serve the People of God by a new and specific title,"[20] with a distinct identity and integrity in the Church that marks him as neither a lay person nor a priest; rather, the deacon is a cleric who is ordained to *diakonia*, namely, a service to God's People in communion with the diocesan bishop and his body of priests. "The principal function of the deacon, therefore, is to collaborate with the bishop and the priests in the exercise of a ministry which is not of their own wisdom but of the Word of God, calling all to conversion and holiness."[21]

31.

Referring to the traditional description of the deacon's *diakonia* to the Church and the diocesan bishop, St. John Paul II observes that in an ancient text, the deacon's ministry is defined as a "service to the bishop."[22] This observation highlights the Church's constant understanding that the deacon enjoys a unique relationship with his diocesan bishop. St. John Paul II clearly has in view, therefore, the reason for not only the diaconate but also the whole apostolic ministry: serving the discipleship of God's People. He notes that the deacon's tasks include that of "promoting and sustaining the apostolic activities of the laity." To the extent that the deacon is more present and more involved than the priest in secular environments and structures, he should feel encouraged to foster closeness between the ordained ministry and lay activities, in common service to the Kingdom of God.[23]

In particular, "a deeply felt need in the decision to reestablish the permanent diaconate," St. John Paul II recalls, "was and is that of a greater and more direct presence of Church ministers in the various spheres of the family, work, school, etc., in addition to existing pastoral structures."[24] The deacon, because of his familiarity with the day-to-day realities and rhythms of the family, neighborhood, and workplace, can relate the rich tradition of Catholic teaching to the practical problems experienced by people. Deacons, both married and celibate, serve God's People by their witness to the gospel value of sacrificial love, a quality of life too easily dismissed in today's society. In their secular employment, deacons also make evident the dignity of human work. Contemporary society is in need of a "new evangelization which demands a greater and more generous effort on the part of [all] ordained ministers."[25] This is especially an opportunity and obligation for deacons in their secular professions to boldly proclaim and witness to the Gospel of life.

32.

In the restoration of the rank of the deacon, the Fathers of the Second Vatican Council described the threefold ministry of deacons: "strengthened by sacramental grace, they are dedicated to the People of God . . . in the service (*diakonia*) of the liturgy, of the Gospel and of works of charity."[26]

> [The deacon] is called to proclaim the Scriptures and instruct and exhort the people. This finds expression in the presentation of the Book of the Gospels, foreseen in the rite of ordination itself. . . . [He is called to] the solemn administration of baptism, in the custody and distribution of the Eucharist, in assisting at and blessing marriages, in presiding at the rites of funeral and burial and in the administration of sacramentals. . . . [Finally, he is called to] dedication to works of charity and assistance and in the direction of communities or sectors of church life.[27]

V.
The Church's Ministry of Word: The Deacon as Evangelizer and Teacher

33.

The deacon participates as an evangelizer and teacher in the Church's mission of heralding the Word. In the Liturgy of the Word, especially in the Eucharist or in other liturgies, the deacon proclaims the Gospel. He may preach by virtue of ordination and in accord with the requirements of canon law.[28] Other forms of the deacon's participation in the Church's ministry of the Word include catechetical instruction; religious formation of candidates and families preparing for the reception of the sacraments; leadership roles in retreats, evangelization, and renewal programs; outreach to alienated Catholics; and counseling and spiritual direction, to the extent that he is properly trained.[29] The deacon also strives to "transmit the word in [his] professional [life] either explicitly or merely by [his] active presence in places where public opinion is formed and ethical norms are applied."[30]

34.

In these and many other formal and informal ways, the deacon leads the community to reflect on its communion and mission in Jesus Christ, especially impelling the community of believers to live lives of service. Because the deacon sacramentalizes service, he should proclaim the Word in such a way that he first witnesses to its empowerment in his own life. By his own faithful practice of the spiritual and corporal works of mercy, the deacon "by word and example . . . should work so that all the faithful, in imitation of Christ, may place themselves at the constant service of their brothers and sisters."[31] In so doing, the deacon can effectively challenge others to live out their baptismal vocation and the consequences of their participation in the Eucharist.

VI.
The Church's Ministry of Liturgy: The Deacon as Sanctifier

35.

For the deacon, as for all members of the Church, the liturgy is "the summit toward which the activity of the Church is directed; at the same time it is the fount from which all the Church's power flows."[32] For the Church gathered at worship, moreover, the ministry of the deacon is a visible, grace-filled sign of the integral connection between sharing at the Lord's eucharistic table and serving the many hungers felt so keenly by all God's children. In the deacon's liturgical ministry, as in a mirror, the Church sees a reflection of her own diaconal character and is reminded of her mission to serve as Jesus did. Pope Francis said during the 2016 Jubilee of Deacons: "when you serve at the table of the Eucharist, there you will find the presence of Jesus, who gives himself to you so that you can give yourselves to others."[33]

36.

In the context of the Church's public worship, because of its centrality in the life of the believing community, the ministry of the deacon in the threefold *diakonia* of the word, of the liturgy, and of charity is uniquely concentrated and integrated. "The diaconate is conferred through a special outpouring of the Spirit (ordination), which brings about in the one who receives it a specific conformation to Christ, Lord and servant of all."[34] "Strengthened by sacramental grace, they are dedicated to the people of God, in conjunction with the diocesan bishop and his body of priests, in a service of the liturgy of the word and of charity."[35]

37.

During the celebration of the eucharistic liturgy, the deacon participates in specific penitential rites as designated in the *Roman Missal.* He properly proclaims the Gospel. He may preach the homily in accord with the provisions of canon law.[36] He voices the needs of the people in the Universal Prayer, needs with which he should have a particular and personal familiarity from the circumstances of his ministry of charity. The deacon assists the presider and other ministers in accepting the offerings of the people—symbolic of his traditional role in receiving and distributing the resources of the community among those in need—and he helps to prepare the gifts for sacrifice. During the celebration he helps the faithful participate more fully, consciously, and actively in the eucharistic sacrifice,[37] may extend the invitation of peace, and serves as an ordinary minister of Holy Communion. Deacons have a special responsibility for the distribution of the chalice. Finally, he dismisses the community at the end of the eucharistic Liturgy. Other liturgical roles for which the deacon is authorized include those of solemnly baptizing, witnessing marriages, bringing *viaticum* to the dying, and presiding over funerals and burials. The deacon can preside at the Liturgies of the Word and communion services in the absence of a priest. He may officiate at celebrations of the Liturgy of the Hours and at exposition and benediction of the Blessed Sacrament. He can conduct public rites of blessing, offer prayer services for the sick and dying, and administer the Church's sacramentals, as designated in the *Book of Blessings*.[38] In the Eastern Catholic Churches, the liturgical ministries of deacons are prescribed by the legislative authority of each particular Church *sui iuris*.

VII.
The Church's Ministry of Charity: The Deacon as Witness and Guide

38.

The deacon's ministry, as St. John Paul II says, "*is the Church's service sacramentalized.*"[39] Therefore, the deacon's service in the Church's ministry of Word and Liturgy would be severely deficient if his exemplary witness and assistance in the Church's ministry of charity did not accompany it. Thus St. John Paul II affirms both: "This is at the very heart of the diaconate to which you have been called: *to be a servant of the mysteries of Christ and, at one and the same time, to be a servant of your brothers and sisters*. That these two dimensions are inseparably joined together in one reality shows the important nature of the ministry which is yours by ordination."[40]

39.

The deacon's service in the Church's ministry of charity is integral to his service in the Church's ministry of Word and Liturgy. "The three contexts of the diaconal ministry . . . represent a unity in service at the level of divine Revelation: the ministry of the word leads to ministry at the altar, which in turn prompts the transformation of life by the liturgy, resulting in charity."[41] "As a [participant] in the one ecclesiastical ministry, [the deacon] is a specific sacramental sign, in the Church, of Christ the Servant. His role is to 'express the needs and desires of the Christian communities' and to be 'a driving force for service, or *diakonia*,' which is an essential part of the mission of the Church."[42] The ancient tradition appears to indicate that, because the deacon was the servant at the table of the poor, he had his distinctive liturgical roles at the Table of the Lord. Similarly, there is a reciprocal correspondence between his role as a herald of the Gospel and his role as an articulator of the needs of the Church in the Universal Prayer. The service of charity is twofold: it is ministering to both the spiritual and physical needs of others. "This charity is both *love of God and love of neighbor*. . . . All around us many of our brothers and sisters live in either *spiritual or material poverty* or both. So many of the world's people are *oppressed by injustice* and the denial of their fundamental human rights. Still others are troubled or suffer from a loss of faith in God, or are tempted to give up hope."[43] Today especially, "the ministry of deacons is particularly valuable, since today the spiritual and material needs of man, to which the Church is called to respond, are greatly diversified."[44] As Pope Benedict XVI reminds us, "Charity is love received and given."[45] The deacon thus symbolizes in his roles the grounding of the Church's life in the Eucharist and the mission of the Church in her loving service. The deacon's service begins at the altar and returns there. The sacrificial love of Christ celebrated in the Eucharist nourishes him and motivates him to lay down his life on behalf of God's People.

40.

The Apostles' decision to appoint ministers to attend to the needs of the Greek-speaking widows of the early Church at Jerusalem (Acts 6:1-7) has long been interpreted as a normative step in the evolution of ministry. It is seen as a practical response to Jesus' command during the Last Supper of mutual service among his followers. In washing his disciples' feet, Jesus as Head and Shepherd of the community modeled the service that he desired to be the hallmark of their faithfulness. This gave the disciples a powerful sign of the love of God that was, in Jesus himself, incarnate and intended to be forever enfleshed in the attitudes and behaviors of his followers (see Jn 13:1-15). The deacon, consecrated and conformed to the mission of Christ, Lord and Servant, has a particular concern for the vitality and genuineness of the exercise of *diakonia* in the life of the believing community. In a world hungry and thirsty for convincing signs of the compassion and liberating love of God, the deacon sacramentalizes the mission of the Church in his words and deeds, responding to the Master's command of service and providing real-life examples of how to carry it out.

VIII.
An Intrinsic Unity

41.

By ordination, the deacon, who sacramentalizes the Church's service, is to exercise the Church's *diakonia*. Therefore, "the diaconal ministries, distinguished above, are not to be separated; the deacon is ordained for them all, and no one should be ordained who is not prepared to undertake each in some way."[46] "However, even if this inherent ministerial service is one and the same in every case, nevertheless, the concrete ways of carrying it out are diverse; these must be suggested, in each case, by the different pastoral situations of the single churches."[47]

A deacon may also have greater abilities in one aspect of ministry; and, therefore, his service may be marked by one of them more than by the others. Fundamentally, however, there is an intrinsic unity in a deacon's ministry. In preaching the Word, he is involved in every kind of missionary outreach. In sanctifying God's People through the Liturgy, he infuses and elevates people with new meaning and with a Christian worldview. In bringing Christ's Reign into every stratum of society, the deacon develops a Christian conscience among all people of good will, motivating their service and commitment to the sanctity of human life.

IX.
Concluding Reflection

42.

When one reflects upon the Order of Deacons, it is worthwhile to recall the words from the Rite of Ordination of Deacons:

> Like those once chosen by the Apostles for the ministry of charity, you should be men of good reputation, filled with wisdom and the Holy Spirit. Firmly rooted and grounded in faith, you are to show yourselves chaste and beyond reproach before God and man, as is proper for the ministers of Christ and the stewards of God's mysteries. Never allow yourselves to be turned away from the hope offered by the Gospel. Now you are not only hearers of this Gospel but also its ministers. Hold the mystery of faith with a clear conscience. Express by your actions the Word of God which your lips proclaim, so that the Christian people, brought to life by the Spirit, may be a pure offering accepted by God. Then on the last day, when you go out to meet the Lord you will be able to hear him say, "Well done, good and faithful servant, enter into the joy of your Lord."[48]

---

[1] BNFPD, no. 3.

[2] LG, no. 1.

[3] LG, no. 17.

[4] LG, no. 8.

[5] LG, no. 8.

[6] LG, no. 8.

[7] LG, no. 8.

[8] CCC, no. 1533.

[9] St. John Paul II, Post-Synodal Apostolic Exhortation *The Vocation and the Mission of the Lay Faithful in the Church and in the World (Christifideles Laici)* (Washington, DC: United States Catholic Conference, 1988), no. 32, citing Acts 1:8.

[10] BNFPD, no. 5.

[11] CCC, no. 1536.

[12] St. John Paul II, *Christifideles Laici*, no. 22. See LG, no. 24.

[13] LG, no. 28.

[14] St. John Paul II, *Christifideles Laici*, no. 22.

[15] Pope Francis, Homily for the Jubilee of Deacons (May 29, 2016).

[16] CCC, no. 1554.

[17] LG, no. 7.

[18] CCC, no. 1570.

[19] St. John Paul II, Post-Synodal Apostolic Exhortation *The Church in America (Ecclesia in America)* (January 22, 1999) (Washington, DC: United States Catholic Conference, 1999), no. 42, citing LG, no. 29.

[20] DMLPD, no. 1. See CIC, c. 1008; Pope Benedict XVI, Omnium in Mentem (October 26, 2009).

[21] DMLPD, no. 23.

[22] St. John Paul II, General Audience "Deacons Have Many Pastoral Functions" (October 13, 1993), no. 1, citing Hippolytus, *Apostolic Tradition*.

[23] St. John Paul II, "Deacons Have Many Pastoral Functions," no. 5, citing St. Paul VI, Apostolic Letter Motu Proprio *Sacrum Diaconatus Ordinem* (June 18, 1967), no. 22, *www.vatican.va/content/paul-vi/en/motu_proprio/documents/hf_p-vi_motu-proprio_19670618_sacrum-diaconatus.html*.

[24] St. John Paul II, General Audience "Deacons Serve the Kingdom of God" (October 5, 1993), no. 6.

[25] DMLPD, no. 26.

[26] See BNFPD, no. 7.

[27] BNFPD, no. 9.

[28] CIC, c. 764: "Without prejudice to the prescript of can. 765, presbyters and deacons possess the faculty of preaching everywhere; this faculty is to be exercised with at least the presumed consent of the rector of the church, unless the competent authority has restricted or taken away the faculty or particular law requires express permission."

[29] See BNFPD, no. 86. To offer psychological counseling, the deacon must receive training in accord with professional standards.

[30] DMLPD, no. 26.

[31] DMLPD, no. 38.

[32] SC, no. 10.

[33] Pope Francis, Homily for the Jubilee of Deacons.

[34] BNFPD, no. 5.

[35] LG, no. 29, cited in PDO.

[36] "Among the forms of preaching, the homily, which is part of the liturgy itself . . . is reserved to a priest or deacon." CIC, c. 767 §1. See also *General Instruction of the Roman Missal*, no. 66.

[37] SC, no. 14.

[38] STVI, 51-57.

[39] ADUS, no. 2, italics original.

[40] ADUS, no. 1, italics original.

[41] DMLPD, no. 39.

[42] BNFPD, no. 5.

[43] ADUS, nos. 3-4, italics original.

[44] DMLPD, no. 38.

[45] Pope Benedict XVI, Encyclical *Charity in Truth (Caritas in Veritate)* (Washington, DC: USCCB, 2009), no. 5.

[46] PDG (1984), no. 43.

[47] BNFPD, no. 10.

[48] Roman Pontifical, Rite of Ordination of Deacons, no. 199, in *Rites of Ordination of a Bishop, of Priests, and of Deacons, Third Typical Edition* (2010). See Mt 25:21.

Chapter Two

The Ministry and Life of Deacons

I.
The Relationships of the Deacon

Relationship with the Diocesan Bishop

43.

THE DEACON EXERCISES HIS MINISTRY within a specific pastoral context: the communion and mission of a diocesan Church.[1] He is in direct relationship with the diocesan bishop with whom he is in communion and under whose authority he is assigned to exercise his ministry. In making his promise of respect and obedience to his diocesan bishop, the deacon takes as his model Christ, who became the Servant of his Father. The diocesan bishop also enters into a relationship with the deacon because the deacon is his collaborator in the service of God's People. It is, therefore, a particular responsibility of the diocesan bishop to provide for the pastoral care of the deacons of his diocese. The diocesan bishop discharges this responsibility both personally and through the Director of the Permanent Diaconate.[2]

44.

The diocesan bishop appoints the deacon to a specific assignment by means of an official letter of appointment.[3] The principal criteria for the assignment are the pastoral needs of the diocesan Church and the personal qualifications of the deacon, as these have been discerned in his previous experience and the course of his initial formation. The assignment also acknowledges the deacon's family and occupational responsibilities.

45.

The diocesan bishop promotes "a suitable catechesis" throughout the diocesan Church to help the lay faithful, religious, and clergy to have a richer and firmer sense about the deacon's identity, function, and role within the Church's ministry.[4] In fact, such a catechesis is also "an opportunity for the bishop, priests, religious, and laity to discern the needs and challenges of the local Church, to consider the types of services needed in order to meet them, to tailor a diaconal program to address them, and to begin the process of considering which men in the church might be called upon to undertake diaconal ministry."[5]

46.

The assignment of a deacon to a specific ministry, the delineation of his duties and responsibilities, and the designation of his immediate pastor or pastoral supervisor, are to be clearly stated in the letter of appointment signed by the diocesan bishop. This document should make as explicit as possible the implicit expectations of the participants, thereby establishing a clear line of mutual responsibility and accountability among them. The Director of the Permanent Diaconate, together with the deacon's designated pastor or priest supervisor (if the deacon is assigned to an office or agency not directed by a priest), a representative of that office or agency, and the deacon are to be involved in the preparation of the letter of appointment. "For the good of the deacon and to prevent improvisation, ordination should be accompanied by clear investiture of pastoral responsibility."[6] Although the wife of a married deacon has already given her consent before her husband's ordination to the demands of the diaconal ministry, nevertheless she should be "kept duly informed of [her husband's] activities in order to arrive at an harmonious balance between family, professional and ecclesial responsibilities."[7] Until the letter of appointment is signed by the diocesan bishop and publicly announced by the diocesan bishop's office, all parties are bound to confidentiality.

47.

The diocesan bishop also ensures that the "rights and duties as foreseen by canons 273-283 of the *Code of Canon Law* with regard to clerics in general and deacons in particular" are promoted.[8]

48.

The transition from the candidate stage of initial formation into an active diaconal ministry requires sensitivity. "Introducing the deacon to those in charge of the community (the parish priest, priests), and the community to the deacon, helps them not only to come to know each other but contributes to a collaboration based on mutual respect and dialogue, in a spirit of faith and fraternal charity."[9] Newly ordained deacons, therefore, are to be appointed to and supervised by a priest. This pastoral care of a newly ordained deacon, coordinated by the Director of the Permanent Diaconate,[10] extends for the first five years after ordination, with a reminder that ongoing formation continues for the entire life of the deacon, until he passes from this life to the next. This time would include opportunities for ongoing formation, with an initial emphasis upon the issues and concerns voiced by the newly ordained as he gains ministerial experience. It is likewise a unique opportunity to assist the deacon's family as it begins to adjust to its new situation within the community.

49.

With the approval of the diocesan bishop, a realistic program for the continuing education and formation of each deacon and the entire diaconal community should be designed "taking due account of factors such as age and circumstances of deacons, together with the demands made on them by their pastoral ministry."[11] The preparation, implementation, and evaluation of this program are to be coordinated by the Director of the Permanent Diaconate. "In addition to the [continuing] formation offered to [all] deacons, special courses and initiatives should be arranged for those deacons who are married," including the participation of their wives and families, "where opportune. . . . However, [care must be given] to maintain the essential distinction of roles and the clear independence of the ministry."[12] Similarly, special initiatives in continuing formation should be arranged for deacons who are not married.

Relationship with the Diocese

50.

While assuming different forms of diaconal ministry, a deacon exercises his service in both a diocesan setting and in an individual assignment. Therefore, he may be given specific responsibility, if he meets the necessary requirements, in an administrative position at a diocesan or parochial level.[13] However, in discharging these administrative responsibilities, "the deacon should recall that every action in the Church should be informed by charity and service to all. . . . Those deacons who are called to exercise such offices should be placed so as to discharge duties which are proper to the diaconate, in order to preserve the integrity of the diaconal ministry."[14]

51.

Deacons who possess the necessary requirements, experience, and talent may be elected or appointed members of the diocesan pastoral council, finance council, or commissions. They may be assigned to diocesan pastoral work in specific social contexts: e.g., the pastoral care of the family or the pastoral needs of ethnic minorities.[15] They may also participate in a diocesan synod.[16] They may exercise the offices of chancellor, judge, assessor, auditor, promoter of justice, defender of the bond, and notary or may serve as the diocesan finance officer.[17] However, deacons do not "act as members of the council of priests, since this body exclusively represents the presbyterate."[18] Deacons may not "be constituted judicial vicars, adjunct judicial vicars, or vicars forane, since these offices are reserved for priests."[19] Deacons are also not permitted to be appointed to the office of moderator of the curia.[20] To strengthen the diaconal character of the diocesan Church, care is to be taken, therefore, to include, as much as possible, a diaconal presence within diocesan structures, as well as within parish communities.[21]

52.

Deacons who have parochial administrative training and experience may be appointed to assist a pastor or team of priests *in solidum* to care for several neighboring parishes.[22] Deacons may also be appointed to participate in the pastoral care of a parish due to a lack of priests.[23] In the latter case, a priest with the powers and faculties of a pastor is to be appointed. Moreover, in such extraordinary situations, deacons "always have precedence over the non-ordained faithful," and their authority and responsibility "should always be clearly specified in writing when they are assigned office."[24]

53.

Where the diocesan bishop has deemed it opportune to institute parish pastoral councils, deacons who exercise pastoral care in a parish are members of the council by right.[25]

Relationship with the Priesthood

54.

Deacons exercise their ministry in communion not only with their diocesan bishop but also with the priests who serve the diocesan Church. As collaborators in ministry, priests and deacons are two complementary but subordinate participants in the one apostolic ministry bestowed by Christ upon the Apostles and their successors. The diaconate is not an abridged or substitute form of the priesthood; it is a full order in its own right.[26] Those who are constituted in the order of the episcopate or the presbyterate receive the mission and capacity to act in the person of Christ the Head, whereas deacons are empowered to serve the People of God in the ministries of the liturgy, the word, and charity.[27]

55.

Priests and deacons are bonded closely together in their common ministry of the Word. All deacons receive the Holy Gospels from the diocesan bishop on their ordination day. This powerful sign of cooperation with the ministry of the diocesan bishop, and its connection to Christ's own mandate (Lk 24:45-49) places the ministry of deacon and priest within a shared communion of obedience to and love of the Word, which together they labor to proclaim. It is laudatory for priests and deacons to deepen their communion, as brothers in Holy Orders, by way of their shared prayer and reflection on the Word of God.[28]

56.

Permanent deacons ought to foster fraternal bonds with transitional deacons. Through formal contacts arranged by the diocesan diaconate and vocation offices with the seminary program, in collaborative diocesan and parochial ministries, and in opportunities for shared study and prayer, the Order of Deacons can more clearly be understood and appreciated among those to be ordained to the Order of Priests.

57.

Deacons and priests, as ordained ministers, should develop a genuine respect for each other, witnessing to the communion and mission they share with one another and with the diocesan bishop in mutual service to the People of God.[29] To foster this communion, the diocese might offer opportunities annually for shared retreats, days of recollection, deanery meetings, continuing education study days, and mutual work on diocesan councils and commissions, as well as regularly scheduled occasions for socialization. Further, the Church's communion and mission "is realized not only by the ministers in virtue of the Sacrament of Orders but also by all the lay faithful."[30] Therefore, the bishop, priests, and deacons need to welcome, inspire, and form the lay faithful to participate in the communion and mission of the Church "because of their Baptismal state and their specific vocation."[31]

58.

Priests are to be aware of the sacramental identity of the deacon, the nature of diaconal spirituality and the specific functions the deacons will perform within the diocesan Church.[32] Priests need to collaborate with the diocesan bishop in planning for the inclusion of deacons within the life and ministry of the diocesan Church. Pastors especially are involved in the presentation, selection, and assessment processes for aspirants and candidates. Priests designated by the diocesan bishop serve as spiritual directors and pastoral supervisors. Priests are expected to catechize the people on the ordained vocation of the deacon and to actively seek out, with the assistance of the parish community, competent nominees for this ministry.[33]

Relationship Among Deacons and Those in Formation

59.

By virtue of their ordination, a sacramental fraternity unites deacons.

They form a community that witnesses to Christ the Deacon-Servant. "Each deacon should have a sense of being joined with his fellow deacons in a bond of charity, prayer, obedience to their bishops, ministerial zeal and collaboration."[34] Therefore, "with the permission of the bishop . . . it would be opportune for deacons periodically to meet to discuss their ministry, exchange experiences, advance formation and encourage each other in fidelity."[35] Canonically, deacons may "form associations among themselves to promote their spiritual life, to carry out charitable and pious works and pursue other objectives which are consonant with their sacramental consecration and mission.[36] However, it must be noted that associations that form as pressure groups that could promote conflict with the diocesan bishop are completely irreconcilable with the clerical state.[37] It may be desirable, therefore, for the diocesan bishop to form a diocesan structure composed of a proportionate number of deacons to coordinate diaconal ministry and life within the diocese.[38] The diocesan bishop would serve as its president and approve its statutes.[39] Finally, the diaconal community should be, for those in the aspirant and candidate stages in formation, "a precious support in the discernment of their vocation, in human growth, in the initiation to the spiritual life, in theological study and pastoral experience."[40]

Relationship with Women and Men Religious

60.

Deacons ought to promote collaboration between themselves and women and men religious who also have dedicated their lives to the service of the Church. Pastoral sensitivity between deacons and religious should be carefully nurtured. Opportunities for dialogue among deacons and religious could serve the Church well in developing and maintaining mutual understanding and support of each other's unique vocation, each of which accomplishes in its own way the common mission of service to the Church.

Relationship with the Laity

61.

By ordination, deacons are members of the clergy.[41] The vast majority of deacons in the United States of America, married or celibate, have secular employment and do not engage exclusively in specific Church-related ministries. This combination of an ordained minister with a secular occupation and personal and family obligations can be a great strength, opportunity, and witness to the laity on how they too might integrate their baptismal call and state in life as they live their Christian faith in society.[42] The deacon likewise enjoys and must exemplify a special collaborative relationship with lay ecclesial ministers and other full-time or part-time professionals who engage in specific Church-related ministries.

62.

The laity, as members of the Church, have an obligation and right to share in the communion and mission of the Church. Through his ordination to service, the deacon promotes, in an active fashion, the various lay apostolates and guides these in communion with the diocesan bishop and local priests.[43] In collaboration with his diocesan bishop and the priests of his diocese, the deacon has a special role to promote communion and to counter the strong emphasis on individualism prevalent in the United States of America. Set aside for service, the deacon links the individual and diverse segments of the community of believers. In his works of charity, the deacon guides and witnesses "the love of Christ for all men instead of personal interests and ideologies which are injurious to the universality of salvation. . . . the *diakonia* of charity necessarily leads to a growth of communion within the particular Churches since charity is the very soul of ecclesial communion."[44]

Relationship with Society

63.

The diaconate is lived in a particularly powerful way in the manner in which a deacon fulfills his obligations to his secular occupation, to his civic and public responsibilities, and among his family and neighbors. This, in turn, enables the deacon to bring back to the Church an appreciation of the meaning and value of the Gospel as he discerns it in the lives and questions of the people he has encountered. In his preaching and teaching, the deacon articulates the needs and hopes of the people he has experienced, thereby animating, motivating, and facilitating a commitment among the lay faithful to an evangelical service in the world.[45]

64.

Specifically, in the third Christian millennium, "the whole Church is called to greater apostolic commitment which is both personal and communitarian, renewed and generous."[46] At the heart of this call is an awareness of a new evangelization: i.e., "to rekindle the faith in the Christian conscience of many and cause the joyful proclamation of salvation to resound in society."[47] The deacon, as herald of the Gospel, has an important pastoral responsibility in the new evangelization.[48] St. John Paul II reminds the Church that "what moves me even more strongly to proclaim the urgency of missionary evangelization is the fact that it is the primary service which the Church can render to every individual . . . in the modern world."[49] The deacon is ordained precisely for service in both the sanctuary and the marketplace.

65.

The secular employment of a deacon is also linked with his ministry.[50] Although his secular work may benefit the community, some professions can become incompatible with the pastoral responsibilities of his ministry. The diocesan bishop, "bearing in mind the requirements of ecclesial communion and of the fruitfulness of pastoral ministry, shall evaluate individual cases as they arise, [and may require] a change of profession after ordination."[51]

Unity in Pastoral Activity

66.

Under the diocesan bishop's authority, joint meetings and cooperative action "arranged between priests, deacons, religious, and laity involved in pastoral work [can] avoid compartmentalization or the development of isolated groups and . . . guarantee coordinated unity for different pastoral activities."[52]

II.
Diaconal Spirituality

Introduction

67.

The primary sources of a deacon's spirituality are his participation in the Sacraments of Christian Initiation, as well as his sacramental identity and participation in ordained ministry. For a deacon who is married, his spirituality is nurtured further in the Sacrament of Matrimony, which sanctifies conjugal love and constitutes it as a sign of the love with which Christ gives himself to the Church. For the celibate deacon, loving God and serving his neighbor roots his whole person in a total and undivided consecration to Christ. For each deacon, his model *par excellence* is Jesus Christ, the Servant who lived totally at the service of his Father for the good of every person.[53] To live their ministry to the fullest, "deacons must know Christ intimately so that He may shoulder the burdens of their ministry."[54] Fundamentally, this knowledge of Christ is given to the deacon as he commits himself to prayerful study of the Word of God. As a man sent by his diocesan bishop to proclaim the Gospel to the poor, the deacon secures this deepest mission by way of fidelity to his deepest identity found only in communion with the living Word (Jn 6:68).

Spiritual Life

68.

Deacons are obligated to give priority to the spiritual life and to live their *diakonia* with generosity. Clerics have a special obligation to seek holiness in their lives "because they are consecrated to God by a new title in the reception of orders as dispensers of God's mysteries in the service of His people."[55] They should integrate their family obligations, professional life, and ministerial responsibilities so as to grow in their commitment to the person and mission of Christ the Servant. A married deacon is encouraged to develop prayer time with his wife and family.

Prayer

69.

The spiritual life cannot be nurtured nor maintained without a habit of prayer. In addition to the requirement that a deacon pray daily the offices of Morning and Evening Prayer of the Liturgy of the Hours, he should foster his love of the Lord through the practice of mental prayer. Blessed Luis of Grenada describes the process: "Once [people] have made some progress in the spiritual life and have acquired some devotion, their love of God prompts them to find ways of expressing their sentiments in a more personal and intimate way. . . . As one's devotion increases, the type of prayer practiced habitually by the individual will likewise rise from vocalized prayer to mental prayer and eventually to contemplation."[56] To help cultivate such a life of prayer, the deacon should reflect daily on Sacred Scripture, employing the steps of *lectio divina* often. If possible, it is recommended that he attend daily Eucharist. The deacon should frequently receive the Sacrament of Penance and devote time to spiritual reading.[57]

Simplicity of Life

70.

Deacons are charged at ordination to shape a way of life always according to the example of Christ and to imitate Christ who came not to be served but to serve. Therefore, deacons are called to a simple lifestyle. Simplicity of life enables a cleric "to stand beside the underprivileged, to practice solidarity with their efforts to create a more just society, to be more sensitive and capable of understanding and discerning realities involving the economic and social aspects of life, and to promote a preferential option for the poor."[58] The prophetic significance of this lifestyle, "so urgently needed in affluent and consumeristic societies,"[59] is its important witness in animating the *diakonia* of every Christian to serve "especially those who are poor or in any way afflicted."[60]

Pastoral Service

71.

As St. John Paul II observes, "A deeply felt need in the decision to reestablish the diaconate was and is that of a greater and more direct presence of Church ministers in the various spheres such as family, work, school, etc., in addition to existing pastoral structures."[61] While transforming the world is the proper role of the laity, the deacon—in communion with his diocesan bishop and the diocesan presbyterate—exhorts, consecrates, and guides the People of God in living faithfully the communion and mission they share in Christ, especially in making the Gospel visible in their daily lives through their concern for justice, peace, and respect for life.[62]

III. The Deacon in His State of Life

The Married Deacon

72.

The majority of deacons in the United States of America are married.[63] These men bring to the Sacrament of Holy Orders the gifts already received and still being nurtured through their participation in the Sacrament of Matrimony.[64] This sacrament sanctifies the love of husbands and wives, making that love an efficacious sign of the love of Christ for his Church. Marriage requires an "interpersonal giving of self, a mutual fidelity, a source of [and openness to] new life, [and] a support in times of joy and sorrow."[65] Lived in faith, this ministry within the domestic Church is a sign to the entire Church of the love of Christ. It forms the basis of the married deacon's unique gift within the Church.[66]

73.

"In particular the deacon and his wife must be a living example of fidelity and indissolubility in Christian marriage before a world which is in dire need of such signs. By facing in a spirit of faith the challenges of married life and the demands of daily living, they strengthen the family life not only of the Church community but of the whole of society. They also show how the obligations of family life, work, and ministry can be harmonized in the service of the Church's mission. Deacons and their wives and children can be a great encouragement to others who are working to promote family life."[67]

74.

A married deacon, with his wife and family, gives witness to the sanctity of marriage. The more they grow in mutual love, conforming their lives to the Church's teaching on marriage and sexuality, the more they give to the Christian community a model of Christlike love, compassion, and self-sacrifice. The married deacon must always remember that through his sacramental participation in both vocational sacraments, first in Matrimony and again in Holy Orders, he is challenged to be faithful to both. With integrity he must live out both sacraments in harmony and balance. The wife of a deacon should be included with her husband, when appropriate, in diocesan clergy and parochial staff gatherings. A deacon and his wife, both as a spiritual man and woman and as a couple, have much to share with the diocesan bishop and his priests about the Sacrament of Matrimony. A diaconal family also brings a unique presence and understanding of the domestic family. "By facing in a spirit of faith the challenges of married life and the demands of daily living, [the married deacon and his family] strengthen the family life not only of the Church community but of the whole of society."[68]

The Celibate Deacon

75.

The Church acknowledges the gift of celibacy that God grants to certain of its members who wholeheartedly live it "*according to its true nature* and according to its real purposes, that is for evangelical, spiritual and pastoral motives."[69] The essential meaning of celibacy is grounded in Jesus' preaching of the Kingdom of God. Its deepest source is love of Christ and dedication to his mission. "In celibate life, indeed, love becomes a sign of total and undivided consecration to Christ and of greater freedom to serve God and man. The choice of celibacy is not an expression of contempt for marriage nor of flight from reality but a special way of serving man and the world."[70]

76.

The celibate commitment remains one of the most fundamental expressions of Jesus' call to radical discipleship for the sake of the Kingdom on earth and as an eschatological sign of the Kingdom of Heaven.[71] "This perfect continency, out of desire for the kingdom of heaven, has always been held in particular honor in the Church. The reason for this was and is that perfect continency for the love of God is an incentive to charity, and is certainly a particular source of spiritual fecundity in the world."[72]

77.

If the celibate deacon gives up one kind of family, he gains another. In Christ, the people he serves become mother, brother, and sister. In this way, celibacy as a sign and motive of pastoral charity takes flesh. Reciprocity, mutuality, and affection shared with many become channels that mold and shape the celibate deacon's pastoral love and his sexuality. "Celibacy should not be considered just as a legal norm . . . but rather as a value . . . whereby [the celibate deacon] takes on the likeness of Jesus Christ . . . as a full and joyful availability in his heart for the pastoral ministry."[73]

Celibacy Affects Every Deacon

78.

In one way or another, celibacy affects every deacon, married or unmarried. Understanding the nature of celibacy—its value and its practice—is essential to the married deacon. Not only does this understanding strengthen and nurture his own commitment to marital chastity, but it also helps to prepare him for the possibility of living celibate chastity should his wife predecease him. Tragically, some deacons who were married at the time of ordination only begin to face the issues involved with celibacy upon the death of their wives. As difficult as this process is, all deacons need to appreciate the impact celibacy can have on their lives and ministry.

The Widowed Deacon

79.

The death of a married deacon's wife is a "particular moment in life which calls for faith and Christian hope."[74] The death of the wife of a married deacon introduces a new reality into the daily routine of his family and ministry. Charity should be extended to the widowed deacon as he assesses and accepts his new personal circumstances, so he will not neglect his primary duty as father to his children or any new needs his family might have.[75] As required, a widowed deacon should be helped to seek professional counsel, and he is always encouraged to address the challenges he faces during the bereavement process with his spiritual director. Further, the fraternal closeness of his diocesan bishop, the priests with whom he ministers, and the diaconal community should offer comfort and reassurance in this difficult moment in his life.[76] "In particular, the widowed deacon should be supported in living perfect and perpetual continence. He should be helped to understand the profound ecclesial reasons which preclude his remarriage (1 Tm 3:12), in accordance with the constant discipline of the Church in the East and West. This can be achieved through an intensification of one's dedication to others for the love of God in the ministry. In such cases the fraternal assistance of other ministers, of the faithful and of the bishop can be most comforting to widowed deacons."[77]

80.

In exceptional cases, the Holy See, having heard the opinion of the deacon's diocesan bishop, may grant a dispensation for a new marriage[78] or for a release from the obligations of the clerical state. However, to ensure a mature decision in discerning God's will, effective pastoral care should be provided to maintain that a proper and sufficient period of time has elapsed before either of these dispensations is sought. If a dispensation for a new marriage is petitioned and granted, the new wife's written informed consent to his exercise of diaconal ministry should be sought before the marriage. Additional time will be required for the formation of a stable relationship in the new marriage; therefore, a suitable period of time is required before the deacon resumes active ministry.

81.

A similar sensitivity also should be given to the widow of a deacon, because she shared so intimately in her husband's life and ministerial witness. The diocesan bishop and her pastor, as well as the diaconal and parish communities, should extend appropriate and adequate support in her bereavement. Widows of deacons ought to remain connected with the diaconal community, not only because of support and encouragement, but because of the unique bonds that had been forged by virtue of her husband's ordination.

A Deacon and Family Confronting Divorce

82.

If a divorce between a deacon and his wife happens, suitable pastoral care should be offered to the deacon, his wife, and their children. This pastoral care, which may be facilitated by the Director of the Permanent Diaconate or any other qualified person on behalf of the diocesan bishop, should include ample time to work through the various stages of grieving and adjustment caused by divorce. The determination of the divorced deacon's ministerial status will require sensitivity and prudence on the part of the diocesan bishop, the pastor or pastoral supervisor, the ministerial community, and other institutions in which the deacon serves. After such beneficial consultation, it is the responsibility of the diocesan bishop then to determine the divorced deacon's ministerial status, in accord with the principles and procedures outlined in paragraph 44, above. Members of the diaconal community are also in a unique position to reach out, as appropriate, in order to help the divorced couple and family deal with the challenges the divorce may entail.

IV.
The Permanency of the Order of Deacons

83.

Underlying the restoration and renewal of the diaconate at the Second Vatican Council was the principle that the diaconate is a stable and permanent rank of ordained ministry. Since the history of the order over the last millennium, however, has centered on the diaconate as a transitory stage leading to the priesthood, actions that may obfuscate the stability and permanence of the order should be minimized. This would include the ordination of celibate or widowed deacons to the priesthood. "Hence ordination [of a permanent deacon] to the Priesthood . . . must always be a very rare exception, and only for special and grave reasons. . . . Given the exceptional nature of such cases, the diocesan bishop should consult the [Congregation for the Clergy] with regard to the intellectual and theological preparation of the candidate, and also . . . the program of priestly formation and the aptitude of the candidate to the priestly ministry."[79]

V.
The Obligations and Rights of Deacons

Incardination

84.

"Through the imposition of hands and the prayer of consecration, [the deacon] is constituted a sacred minister and a member of the hierarchy."[80] Having already clearly expressed in writing his intention to serve the diocesan Church for life, upon his ordination the deacon is incardinated into the diocesan Church. "Incardination is a juridical bond. It has ecclesiastical and spiritual significance in as much as it expresses the ministerial dedication of the deacon to a specific diocesan Church."[81] The permanent deacon should be familiar with the universal law governing incardination and excardination, as expressed in the *Code of Canon Law*, canons 265 through 272.

The Church's Ministry of the Word

85.

As a participant in the Church's ministry of the word, the deacon heeds the charge given him at ordination: "Receive the Gospel of Christ, whose herald you now are. Believe what you read, teach what you believe, and practice what you teach."[82] The deacon must always remain a student of God's Word, for only when the Word is deeply rooted in his own life can he bring that Word to others.[83] The deacon ought to remember that his actions and public pronouncements involve the Church and its Magisterium. Therefore, he is obligated to cherish the communion and mission that bind him to the Holy Father and his own diocesan bishop, especially in his preaching of Scripture, the Creed, Catholic teachings, and the disciplines of the Church.[84]

86.

Deacons are ordained "to proclaim the Gospel and preach the Word of God."[85] They "have the faculty to preach everywhere, in accordance with the conditions established by [canon law]."[86] "Deacons should be trained carefully to prepare their homilies in prayer, in study of the sacred texts, in perfect harmony with the Magisterium and in keeping with the [age, culture, and abilities] of those to whom they preach."[87] Further, "by their conduct . . . by transmitting Christian doctrine and by devoting attention to the problems of our time . . . [deacons] collaborate with the bishop and the priests in the exercise of a ministry which is not of their wisdom but of the Word of God, calling all to conversion and holiness."[88]

87.

Deacons are obliged to submit to their local ordinary for permission to publish any written materials concerning faith and morals.[89] The permission of the local ordinary is required before writings are submitted to newspapers, magazines, or periodicals.[90] Deacons are required to adhere to the norms established by the USCCB when participating in radio or television broadcasts and must adhere to diocesan policies when participating in public media and in discourse on the Internet.[91]

The Church's Ministry of Liturgy

88.

As an ordained participant in the Church's ministry of Liturgy, the deacon confirms his identity as servant of the Body of Christ. In the celebration of the sacraments, whether he serves as a presider or assists the presider, "let him remember that, when lived with faith and reverence, these actions of the Church contribute much to growth in the spiritual life and to the increase of the Christian community."[92]

89.

Deacons, in communion with the diocesan bishop and priests, serve in the sanctification of the Christian community. "In the Eucharistic Sacrifice, the deacon does not celebrate the mystery: rather, he effectively represents on the one hand, the people of God and, specifically, helps them to unite their lives to the offering of Christ; while on the other, in the name of Christ himself, he helps the Church to participate in the fruits of that sacrifice."[93] While exercising his liturgical ministries, "the deacon is to observe faithfully the rubrics of the liturgical books without adding, omitting or changing of his own volition what they require. . . . For the Sacred Liturgy they should vest worthily and with dignity, in accordance with the prescribed liturgical norms. The dalmatic, in its appropriate liturgical colors, together with the alb, cincture and stole, 'constitutes the liturgical dress proper to deacons.'"[94] Specific liturgical functions of the deacon in the Latin Rite of the Catholic Church are contained in chapter one of this *National Directory*.

The Church's Ministry of Charity

90.

As an ordained participant in the Church's ministry of charity, the deacon assumes the duties entrusted to him by his diocesan bishop with humility and enthusiasm. At the core of his spirituality, a deacon puts on Christ and is guided by the love of Christ in caring for all in his charge: "Charity is the very soul of ecclesial communion."[95] This charity is universal, and the deacon looks to human need in its broadest sense. The deacon is to cultivate an imagination that takes him to the heart of human need. In a real sense the ministry of a deacon is not limited to any particular service; instead his missionary service is agile and deliberative. The deacon is attentive to human pain in all its forms as he discerns that portion of the Gospel to be poured into the wounds of human suffering (Lk 10:34). As Pope Benedict XVI noted, "In these years new forms of poverty have emerged. . . . Beside material poverty, we also find spiritual and cultural poverty. . . . Be servants of the Truth in order to be messengers of the joy that God desires to give to every human being."[96] As a man sent from the diocesan bishop in the name of Christ the Servant, the deacon holds within his heart a vision of charity as wide and deep as the one held in the heart of Christ.

91.

In the prayer of diaconal ordination, the diocesan bishop implores God that the deacon may be "full of all the virtues, sincere in charity, solicitous towards the weak and the poor, humble in their service . . . [and] may . . . be the image of your Son who did not come to be served but to serve."[97] Therefore, "by word and example," the deacon places himself "at the constant service of [his] brothers and sisters."[98] This service includes diocesan and parochial works of charity, including the Church's concern for social justice. It also extends into Christian formation—working with youth and adults and transforming the world through personal witness in conformity with the Gospel of life and justice. The deacon must strive, therefore, to serve all of humanity "without discrimination, while devoting particular care to the suffering and the sinful."[99] Ultimately, the deacon's principal *diakonia*—a sign of the Church's mission—"should bring [all whom he serves] to an experience of God's love and move [them] to conversion by opening [their] heart[s] to the work of grace."[100]

Age for Ordination

92.

In accord with canon law,[101] the USCCB establishes the minimum age for ordination to the permanent diaconate at thirty-five for all candidates, married or celibate. The establishment of a maximum age for ordination is at the discretion of the diocesan bishop, keeping in mind the particular needs and expectations of the diocese regarding diaconal ministry and life.

Clerical Title

93.

Although various forms of address have emerged with regard to deacons, the Congregation for the Clergy has determined that in all forms of address for permanent deacons, the appropriate title is "Deacon."[102]

Clerical Attire

94.

The *Code of Canon Law* does not oblige permanent deacons to wear an ecclesiastical garb.[103] Further, because they are prominent and active in secular professions and society, the USCCB specifies that permanent deacons should resemble the lay faithful in dress and matters of lifestyle. Each diocesan bishop should, however, determine and promulgate any exceptions to this law, as well as specify the appropriate clerical attire if it is to be worn.

Liturgy of the Hours

95.

Permanent deacons in the United States of America are required to include as part of their daily prayer those parts of the Liturgy of the Hours known as Morning and Evening Prayer.[104] Permanent deacons are obliged to pray for the universal Church. Whenever possible, they should lead these prayers with the community to whom they have been assigned to minister.

Participation in Political Office

96.

A deacon may not present his name for election to any public office or in any other general election, or accept a nomination or an appointment to public office, without the prior written permission of the diocesan bishop.[105] A deacon may not actively and publicly participate in another's political campaign without the prior written permission of the diocesan bishop.

Temporary Absence from an Assignment

97.

Deacons may temporarily absent themselves from their place of assignment only with the permission of their proper pastor and/or supervisor. Absences of more than thirty days' duration must be approved by the proper local ordinary.[106]

Letter of Appointment

98.

A deacon shall receive a letter of appointment from his diocesan bishop, which includes the designation of his immediate pastor and/or supervisor.

99.

The diocesan bishop may assign a deacon to assist a pastor entrusted with the pastoral care of one or several parishes.[107]

Support of the Clergy

100.

Permanent deacons are to take care of their own and their family's financial needs (e.g., housing, health insurance, retirement) using income derived from their full-time employment by the diocese, parish, or secular profession.[108] In an individual situation of need, the diocesan Church is to see that the deacon and his family do not lack the basic necessities of life.

Social Security Insurance

101.

To provide for their own upkeep, every permanent deacon should satisfy the legal requirements for Social Security benefits or a comparable program.[109]

Remuneration

102.

Permanent deacons in full-time employment by the diocese, parish, or agency are to receive remuneration commensurate with the salaries and benefits provided to the lay men and women on staff for that particular occupation.[110]

103.

In accordance with diocesan policy, permanent deacons in full-time secular employment, as well as those in part-time ministries, are to be reimbursed for legitimate expenses incurred in their ministry.[111]

Continuing Formation and Spiritual Retreat

104.

Deacons are entitled to a period of time each year for continuing education and spiritual retreat.[112] Norms should be established in each diocese regarding the suitable length of time for these activities and the manner in which the deacon shall receive financial assistance for his expenses either from the diocese, from the current place of ministerial service, or from a combination of sources. The responsibility for covering ongoing formation expenses should be treated similarly for all clerics in pastoral ministry in the diocese.

Financial Assistance to Those in Formation

105.

The diocesan bishop is to determine the financial assistance, if any, that is to be provided to inquirers, as well as to those enrolled in the aspirant stage of diaconal formation. For those admitted into the candidate stage of formation for the diaconate, some financial assistance, at least partial, should be provided for educational needs (e.g., tuition, books, tapes) and for mandatory aspects of formation (e.g., required retreats, workshops). Policies should be established and followed consistently in each diocese regarding the parties (for example, the diocese, the parish, and the candidate) who are responsible for formation expenses.

Loss of Diaconal Status

106.

A deacon can lose the clerical state by canonical dismissal or by a rescript granted by the Holy See. Deacons who lose the clerical state are no longer bound by the obligations arising from Holy Orders and do not enjoy the rights, offices, functions, and powers accorded clerics in the Church.

Withdrawal of Diaconal Faculties

107.

If the ministry of a permanent deacon becomes ineffective or even harmful due to some personal difficulties or irresponsible behavior, his ministerial assignment and/or faculties are to be withdrawn by the diocesan bishop in accord with canon law.

Diocesan Liability

108.

The diocesan bishop must provide for insurance regarding the liability of the diocese for actions taken by a permanent deacon in the course of his public official ministry. The same policies that govern liability for priests in the diocese are to be applicable to permanent deacons.

Service of a Deacon from Another Diocesan Church

109.

A diocesan bishop is under no obligation to accept a permanent deacon—ordained or incardinated elsewhere—for assignment to a diocesan or parochial ministry. Nevertheless, because a permanent deacon is an ordained cleric, the diocesan bishop may not ordinarily forbid a visiting permanent deacon the exercise of his order, provided that the deacon is in good standing and with due regard for the provisions of particular law.

Bi-Ritual Permanent Deacons

110.

When a permanent deacon of an Eastern Catholic Church *sui iuris* is granted bi-ritual faculties to assist in the Latin Church, he may witness marriages with the proper delegation. If one of the parties to be married, however, is ascribed to an Eastern Catholic Church *sui iuris*, for validity only a properly delegated priest may solemnize the marriage by giving the priestly blessing. When a permanent deacon of the Latin Church is granted bi-ritual faculties to assist in an Eastern Catholic Church *sui iuris*, his exercise of the granted faculties is to be in accord with the prescriptions of the respective Eastern Catholic Church *sui iuris*.

Resignation and Retirement

111.

Norms should be established in each diocese regarding the age, health, and other matters that need to be considered regarding a deacon's resignation from a ministerial office or his retirement from ministerial duties.

Norms

(The number[s] found in parentheses after each norm refer[s] to the appropriate paragraph[s] in this *Directory*.)

1. It is incumbent on the diocesan bishop to provide for the pastoral care of deacons of the diocese. This is discharged personally and through the Director of the Permanent Diaconate, who must always be a cleric. (43)
2. The principal criteria for the assignment of a deacon are the pastoral needs of the diocesan Church and the personal qualifications of

the deacon, as these have been discerned in his previous experience and the course of his formation. (44)

3. When the permanent diaconate is being newly implemented in a diocese, a catechetical introduction to the diaconate should be given to the priests, religious, and laity. (45, 57)
4. Deacon assignments ought to provide ample opportunities for an integrated exercise of the threefold diaconal ministry: word, liturgy, and charity. (46)
5. A program for newly ordained deacons during the first five years of their ministry is to be coordinated and supervised by the Director of the Permanent Diaconate. (48) Under the diocesan bishop's authority, periodic meetings should be arranged between priests, deacons, religious, and laity involved in pastoral work "to avoid compartmentalization or the development of isolated groups and to guarantee coordinated unity for different pastoral activities in the diocese."105 The ongoing formation continues throughout the deacon's earthly life. (48)
6. The deacon must give priority to the spiritual life. As a minister of the liturgy, the deacon confirms his identity as servant of the Body of Christ. (68, 88)
7. The vocation to the permanent diaconate presupposes the stability and permanency of the order. Hence, the ordination of a permanent deacon to the priesthood is always a rare exception, and it must be done in consultation with the Congregation for the Clergy. (83)
8. Deacons have the faculty to preach everywhere, in accordance with the conditions established by canon law. (86)
9. Deacons are obliged to submit to their local ordinary for permission to publish any written materials concerning faith and morals. The permission of the local ordinary is required before writings are submitted to newspapers, magazines, or periodicals. Deacons are required to adhere to the norms established by the USCCB when participating in radio or television broadcasts, and to diocesan policies when participating in public media and the Internet. (87)
10. The minimum age for ordination to the permanent diaconate is thirty-five. The establishment of a maximum age of ordination is at the discretion of the diocesan bishop, keeping in mind both

diocesan needs and expectations of diaconal life and ministry. (92)

11. In all forms of address for permanent deacons, the appropriate title is "Deacon." (93)
12. The *Code of Canon Law* does not oblige permanent deacons to wear an ecclesiastical garb. Further, because they are more prominent and active in secular professions and society, the USCCB specifies that permanent deacons should resemble the lay faithful in dress and matters of lifestyle. Each diocesan bishop should, however, determine and promulgate any exceptions to this law, as well as specify the appropriate clerical attire. (94)
13. Permanent deacons are required to include as part of their daily prayer those parts of the Liturgy of the Hours known as Morning and Evening Prayer. (95)
14. A permanent deacon may not present his name for election to any public office or in any other general election, or accept a nomination or an appointment to public office, without the prior written permission of the diocesan bishop. A permanent deacon may not actively and publicly participate in another's political campaign without the prior written permission of the diocesan bishop. (96)
15. The deacon shall receive an official letter of appointment from his diocesan bishop. (46, 47, 98)
16. Until the decree of appointment is publicly announced by the diocesan bishop's office, all parties are bound to confidentiality. (46)
17. Every permanent deacon should satisfy the legal requirements of Social Security benefits or a comparable program. (101)
18. Deacons in full-time employment by the diocese, parish, or agency are to receive remuneration commensurate with the salaries and benefits provided to the lay men or women on staff for that particular occupation. (102)
19. In accordance with diocesan policy, deacons in full-time secular employment, as well as those in part-time ministries, are to be reimbursed for legitimate expenses incurred in their ministry. (103)
20. For those admitted into the candidate stage of formation, some financial assistance should be provided for educational needs and mandatory aspects of formation. (105)

21. The diocesan bishop must provide for insurance regarding the liability of the diocese for actions taken by a permanent deacon in the course of his public official ministry. The same policies that govern liability for priests in the diocese should be applicable to permanent deacons. (108)
22. Norms should be established in each diocese regarding the age, health, and other matters that need to be considered regarding a deacon's resignation from a ministerial office or his retirement from ministerial duties. (111)

---

[1] DMLPD, nos. 1-2.

[2] DMLPD, nos. 8, 78, 80. See no. 3.

[3] See CIC, cc. 156, 157. DMLPD, no. 8, refers to this written conferral of office as a "decree of appointment."

[4] BNFPD, no. 16.

[5] PDG (1984), no. 51.

[6] DMLPD, no. 40. See also no. 41.

[7] DMLPD, no. 61.

[8] DMLPD, no. 7.

[9] DMLPD, no. 77.

[10] Or other office designated by the diocesan bishop.

[11] DMLPD, nos. 78-79.

[12] DMLPD, no. 81. See also no. 60 regarding the needs of celibate deacons.

[13] DMLPD, no. 41.

[14] DMLPD, no. 42.

[15] DMLPD, no. 42.

[16] DMLPD, no. 42. See CIC, c. 463 §2.

[17] DMLPD, nos. 38, 42. See CIC, cc. 482, 483, 494, 1421, 1425 §4, 1428, 1430, 1432.

[18] DMLPD, no. 42.

[19] DMLPD, no. 42.

[20] CIC, c. 473 §2.

[21] DMLPD, nos. 41-42.

[22] CIC, cc. 526 §1; 517 §1.

[23] CIC, c. 517 §2.

[24] DMLPD, no. 41. See CIC, c. 517 §2; Congregation for the Clergy et al., *Instruction on Certain*

Questions Regarding the Collaboration of the Non-Ordained Faithful in the Sacred Ministry of Priest (August 15, 1997), art. 4 §1a, *www.vatican.va/roman_curia/pontifical_councils/laity/documents/rc_con_interdic_doc_15081997_en.html*; and Congregation for the Clergy, Instruction *The Priest, Pastor and Leader of the Parish Community* (August 4, 2002), art. 25, *www.vatican.va/roman_curia/congregations/cclergy/documents/rc_con_cclergy_doc_20020804_istruzione-presbitero_en.html.*

[25] DMLPD, no. 41; CIC, c. 536.

[26] DMLPD, nos. 1, 41.

[27] CIC, c. 1009 §3.

[28] "We, ordained ministers, have received from the Lord, through the mediation of the Church, the task of preaching the Word of God to the ends of the earth. . . . To know Revelation, to adhere unconditionally to Jesus Christ as a fascinated and enamored disciple . . . this is . . . what awaits a permanent deacon, decisively and without any reservation. From a good disciple a good missionary is born. The ministry of the Word . . . requires of ordained ministers a constant struggle to study it and carry it out, at the same time as one proclaims it to others. . . . Lectio divina, that is, prayerful reading, is one much counseled way to understand and live the Word of God, and make it one's own." Cardinal Claudio Hummes, Prefect of the Congregation for the Clergy, August 10, 2009.

[29] DMLPD, especially no. 37.

[30] St. John Paul II, *On the Vocation and the Mission of the Lay Faithful in the Church and in the World* (*Christifideles Laici*) (Washington, DC: United States Catholic Conference, 1988), no. 23.

[31] St. John Paul II, *Christifideles Laici*, no. 23.

[32] "Ordinaries . . . to whom the present document is given, [should] ensure that it becomes an object of attentive reflection in communion with their priests and communities." BNFPD, no. 90.

[33] BNFPD, no. 16.

[34] DMLPD, no. 6.

[35] DMLPD, no. 6.

[36] DMLPD, no. 11; see CIC, c. 278.

[37] DMLPD, no. 11.

[38] DMLPD, no. 80.

[39] DMLPD, no. 80.

[40] BNFPD, no. 26.

[41] DMLPD, nos. 1, 7.

[42] DMLPD, no. 73.

[43] See St. John Paul II, General Audience "Deacons Have Many Pastoral Functions" (October 13, 1993), no. 5.

[44] DMLPD, no. 55.

[45] DMLPD, no. 43. See also nos. 25-27.

[46] Congregation for the Clergy, *The Priest and the Third Christian Millennium* (Washington, DC: United States Catholic Conference, 1999), introduction.

[47] Congregation for the Clergy, *Priest and the Third Christian Millennium*, introduction.

[48] DMLPD, no. 26.

[49] RM, no. 2.

[50] DMLPD, no. 12.

[51] DMLPD, no. 12.

[52] DMLPD, no. 78.

[53] BNFPD, no. 11.

[54] DMLPD, no. 50.

[55] CIC, c. 276 §1.

[56] Luis of Grenada, *Pathways to Holiness*, trans. and adapt. Jordan Aumann, OP (New York: Alba, 1998), 107.

[57] See, for example, CIC, c. 276.

[58] PDV, no. 30.

[59] PDV, no. 30.

[60] GS, no. 1.

[61] St. John Paul II, General Audience "Deacons Serve the Kingdom of God" (October 5, 1993), no. 6.

[62] ADUS.

[63] NSD (1996) reports that 97 percent of all deacons in the United States are married (2).

[64] See paragraph 178 in this text regarding those who are in a mixed marriage or a non-sacramental marriage.

[65] DMLPD, no. 61.

[66] DMLPD, no. 61.

[67] ADUS.

[68] ADUS, no. 5.

[69] PDV, no. 50, italics original.

[70] DMLPD, no. 60.

[71] LG, no. 42.

[72] LG, no, 42; see Roman Pontifical, Rite of Ordination of Deacons, no. 199, in *Rites of Ordination of a Bishop, of Priests, and of Deacons, Third Typical Edition* (2010).

[73] PDV, no. 50.

[74] DMLPD, no. 62.

[75] DMLPD, no. 62.

[76] DMLPD, no. 62.

[77] DMLPD, no. 62.

[78] DMLPD, note 193, citing Congregation for Divine Worship and the Discipline of the Sacraments, Circular Letter, Prot. No. 263/97 (June 6, 1997), no. 8. See also Congregation for Divine Worship and the Disciple of the Sacraments, Letter, Prot. No. 1080/05 (July 13, 2005). Competency for such dispensations belongs to the Congregation for the Clergy. The Congregation will take into consideration only exceptional cases involving personal and diocesan necessity.

[79] DMLPD, no. 5.

[80] DMLPD, no. 1.

[81] DMLPD, no. 2; see Bishops' Committee on the Diaconate, NCCB, *Protocol for the Incardination/Excardination of Permanent Deacons* (1995, revised 1999).

[82] Roman Pontifical, Rite of Ordination of Deacons, p. 171.

[83] St. Augustine, *Serm.* 179, no. 1.

[84] DMLPD, no. 23.

[85] DMLPD, no. 24.

[86] DMLPD, no. 24. See also CIC, c. 764, cited in no. 33 of this *National Directory*.

[87] DMLPD, no. 25.

[88] DMLPD, no. 23.

[89] DMLPD, no. 26.

[90] See CIC, c. 831 §1.

[91] DMLPD, no. 26. See CIC, c. 772 §2; and complementary legislation from the United States Conference of Catholic Bishops, "Canon 772, §2—Radio or TV Talks on Christian Doctrine," *www.usccb.org/beliefs-and-teachings/what-we-believe/canon-law/complementary-norms/canon-772-2-norm-for-giving-radio-or-tv-talks-on-christian-doctrine*. The United States Conference of Catholic Bishops' complementary norms apply only to talks given on radio or television.

[92] DMLPD, no. 53.

[93] DMLPD, no. 28.

[94] DMLPD, no. 30.

[95] DMLPD, no. 55.

[96] Pope Benedict XVI, Address to the Permanent Deacons of Rome (February 18, 2006), *www.vatican.va/content/benedict-xvi/en/speeches/2006/february/documents/hf_ben-xvi_spe_20060218_deacons-rome.html*.

[97] DMLPD, no. 38, citing Pontificale Romanum, *De Ordinatione Episcopi, Presbyterorum et Diaconorum*, no. 207.

[98] DMLPD, no. 38.

[99] DMLPD, no. 38.

[100] DMLPD, no. 38.

[101] See CIC, c. 1031 §3.

[102] "The introduction of the title 'Reverend Mr.' for permanent deacons could further complicate the issue of identity for deacons. The term 'Reverend' has traditionally been associated with priests and used only for transitional deacons on their way to priesthood. As there is great sensitivity surrounding the issue of a deacon being seen as a 'mini-priest,' it would seem that the title 'Reverend Mr.' would lead to continued identification of the diaconate with the priesthood, rather than contributing to the independence and integrity of the Order of Deacon in itself. The title 'Deacon' would, of course, be appropriate." Congregation for Catholic Education and the Congregation for the Clergy, *Joint Study of the US Draft Document–The National Directory for the Formation, Ministry and Life of Permanent Deacons in the United States*, Prot. No. 78/2000 (March 4, 2002).

[103] CIC, c. 288.

[104] CIC, c. 276 §2 3°.

[105] DMLPD, no. 13. See CIC, cc. 285 §3, 288. The rationale is that the identity of a political candidate becomes well known, and any investigation regarding background or reputation of the deacon should be the responsibility of ecclesial authorities so as to avoid any undue or unwarranted publicity in the public media. In making his determination to grant written permission, the bishop should investigate the background of the deacon, including his many social relationships (e.g., memberships in clubs, organizations) so that nothing would become an embarrassment to the Church. The bishop should investigate the credit rating of the deacon so that there is no question of unreasonable indebtedness. He also should be concerned about fundraising that the deacon, as a political candidate, will have to initiate, as well as improper reflections that might occur by associating the deacon, as a political candidate, with a particular party and its platform.

[106] See CIC, c. 283 §1.

[107] DMLPD, no. 41. See also no. 40.

[108] CIC, c. 281 §3.

[109] DMLPD, no. 15; see CIC, cc. 281, 1274.

[110] DMLPD, no. 16.

[111] DMLPD, no. 20. Possible examples include videos for baptismal preparation programs, handouts, refreshments for required gatherings, and distinctive clerical garb. It also could include reimbursement for the personal use of and gasoline for his car in ministry, using IRS mileage standards and records. Note that these are only examples; diocesan policies determine parameters and policies that address the particular reimbursements for deacons.

[112] CIC, c. 276 §2 4°.

Chapter Three

Dimensions in the Formation of Deacons

I.
Introduction

112.

THREE SEPARATE BUT INTEGRAL STAGES constitute a unified diocesan formation program for deacons: the two initial formation stages of aspirant and candidate, and the post-ordination stage of ongoing formation. Although this *National Directory* addresses each stage separately, they nevertheless become "one sole organic journey" in diaconal formation.[1] In each stage, the four dimensions or specific areas in formation—human, spiritual, intellectual, and pastoral—are always essential.[2]

II.
Dimensions of Formation

113.

One who will serve as a deacon requires a formation that promotes the development of the whole person. Therefore, the four dimensions in formation should be so interrelated as to achieve a continual integration of their objectives in the life of each participant and in his exercise of ministry.[3]

Human Dimension

114.

A participant comes to initial formation with a history of interrelationships with other people. Initial formation for ministry begins with human formation and development. Participants "should therefore cultivate a series of human qualities, not only out of proper and due growth and realization of self, but also with a view to the ministry."

Human Dimension Objectives

115.

Deacons have an important role to support the role of the laity in the field of human development. The glory of the lay person is the transformation of culture. "Since the laity, in accordance with their state of life, live in the midst of the world and its concerns, they are called by God to exercise their apostolate in the world like leaven, with the ardor of the spirit of Christ."[4] In catechizing, preaching, and counseling the deacon motivates, facilitates, and animates the laity in their apostolate in the world. In proclaiming God's Word, the deacon evangelizes the believer and unbeliever alike. And "as a minister at the altar . . . [he will] give the Lord's body and blood to the community of believers."[5] The deacon collaborates with the diocesan bishop in the latter's responsibility for catechesis in the local Church.[6] The Congregation for the Evangelization of Peoples, in its *Guide for Catechists*, offers the following attributes for catechists that apply equally to deacons:

a. "in the **purely human sphere**: psychophysical equilibrium—good health, a sense of responsibility, honesty, dynamism; good professional and family conduct, a spirit of sacrifice, strength, perseverance"
b. "with a view to the **functions of a . . . [deacon]**: good human relations, ability to dialogue with those of other religions, grasp of one's own culture, ability to communicate, willingness to work with others, leadership qualities, balanced judgment, openness of mind, a sense of realism, a capacity to transmit consolation and hope"
c. "with a view to **particular situations or roles**: aptitudes for working in the fields of peacemaking, development, socio-cultural promotion, justice, health care"[7]

To this list may be added other important qualities, such as the ability to manage conflict, collaborate, and organize, always contributing to the unity of the parish.

116.

The Congregation for Catholic Education's *Basic Norms for the Formation of Permanent Deacons* highlights four aspects of human maturity that must be considered when developing initial formation programs for deacons. These include the following: (1) formation in the human virtues, (2) the capacity to relate to others, (3) affective maturity (including psychosexual maturity and health), and (4) training in freedom, which "includes the education of the moral conscience."[8] Deacons, above all, must be persons who can relate well to others.[9] This ability flows from an affective maturity that "presupposes . . . the victorious struggle against their own selfishness."[10] Mature ways of relating to others are important servant-leadership qualities. Those who aspire to this ministry need to collaborate well with others and to confront challenges in a constructive way. "A precondition for an authentic human maturity is training in freedom, which is expressed in obedience to the truth of one's own being."[11]

117.

Human formation aims to enhance the personality of the minister in such a way that he becomes "a bridge and not an obstacle for others in their meeting with Jesus Christ."[12] Accordingly, formation processes need to be structured so as to nurture and encourage the participants "to acquire and perfect a series of human qualities which will permit them to enjoy the trust of the community, to commit themselves with serenity to the pastoral ministry, to facilitate encounter and dialogue."[13] Therefore, all of these various aspects of human maturity must be carefully considered when planning the formation program and when assessing a participant's effective integration of them. Directors should acknowledge and be aware of age-appropriate affective and moral development in middle-aged men. If warranted, a participant may also consult (or be asked to do so) with a qualified professional, approved by the director of formation, to assist in this assessment. Every participant for the diaconate should be aware of his own life history and be ready to share these with his formator. It may not be possible for each diocesan director to serve as personal formator due to the numbers of men in initial formation. Formators should be properly trained themselves so as to assist the men in formation with developing self-knowledge and growing in moral and emotional freedom. Such formators, ideally deacons, should be specifically trained to guide participants in honestly assessing the state of their marriages, their emotional and moral life, their work life, and their relations with their pastor and how these affect their capacity to fully enter formation.

Spiritual Dimension

118.

"Human formation leads to and finds its completion in the spiritual dimension of formation, which constitutes the heart and unifying center of every Christian formation. Its aim is to tend to the development of the new life received in Baptism."[14] "Being Christian is not the result of an ethical choice or a lofty idea, but the encounter with an event, a person, which gives life a new horizon and a decisive direction."[15] The spiritual life is, therefore, dynamic and never static. The first goal of initial spiritual formation is the establishment and nourishment of attitudes, habits, and practices that will set the foundation for a lifetime of ongoing spiritual discipline.

119.

A man should not be admitted to initial diaconal formation unless it is demonstrated that he is already living a life of mature Christian spirituality.[16] Such maturity is evidenced by a habit of prayer, especially praying with Scripture, a strong habit of attending Mass that goes beyond the fulfillment of the obligation,[17] and a commitment to ongoing spiritual reading. A love of the Word of God is crucial for anyone who considers himself called to proclaim the Gospel at Mass and other liturgies. The spiritual dimension of formation should "affirm and strengthen" this spirituality, and it should emphasize "specific traits of diaconal spirituality."[18] These specific traits are directly related to the deacon's being a servant after the example of Christ. As an ordained minister living in the world, the deacon's spirituality is tied to his activity in the world, bringing others to Christ and his Church.

120.

Configured sacramentally to Christ the Servant, a deacon's spirituality must be grounded in the attitudes of Christ. These include "simplicity of heart, total giving of self and disinterest for self, humble and helpful love for the brothers and sisters, especially the poorest, the suffering and the most needy, the choice of a lifestyle of sharing and poverty."[19] This diaconal spirituality is nourished by the Eucharist, which, "not by chance, characterizes the ministry of the deacon."[20] A diaconal spirituality is conditioned by participation in the apostolic ministry and should be marked by openness to God's Word, to the Church, and to the world.[21] The fundamental spiritual attitude should be one of openness to this Word contained in Revelation, as preached by the Church, celebrated in the Liturgy, and lived out in the lives of God's People. In these ways, with the assistance of a spiritual director, a man takes on the heart and mind of a deacon. Being configured to Christ the Servant (Lk 10:29 ff.; 14:15-23; 17:7-10; 22:27), each participant begins to think and choose and discern anew. It is Christ the Servant who is now the compelling figure in a candidate's life, affecting him with a different mind and a new desire to remain with Christ in prayer. Prayer will open the participant to a missionary zeal, one needed for the deacon to herald the new evangelization—bringing God's love and salvation to all in word and action. The preaching of the Word is always connected, therefore, with prayer, the celebration of the Eucharist, and the building of community. The earliest community of Christ's disciples was a model of this (see Acts, chapters 2–4; see also 1:14). To attain an interior spiritual maturity requires an intense sacramental and prayer life.

Spiritual Dimension Objectives

121.

The objectives of the spiritual dimension in formation are as follows:

a. To deepen the deacon's prayer life—personal, familial, communal, and liturgical—with special emphasis on participation in Eucharist, daily if possible; daily celebration of the Liturgy of the Hours, especially Morning and Evening Prayer; *lectio divina*; devotion to the

Blessed Virgin Mary and the saints; and regular reception of the Sacrament of Penance

b. To help the participant, with the help of his spiritual director and those responsible for formation, to deepen and cultivate a service commitment to God's Word, the Church, and the world
c. To acquaint him with the Catholic spiritual Tradition reflected in classic spiritual writings and in the lives of the saints, and with contemporary developments in spirituality—a faith seeking to be expressed and celebrated
d. To affirm the Christian witness of matrimonial and celibate spirituality
e. To incarnate his spirituality in the real life and history of the people whom he encounters each day in places where he lives, works, and serves[22]

122.

Discernment is an essential spiritual process in determining the presence of a vocation to the diaconate, as well as the capacity to live it fully after ordination. The spiritual dimension of formation, therefore, should assist the participant in assessing the depth and quality of his integration of personal, family, employment, and ministerial responsibilities. Further, it should assist his growth in self-knowledge, in his commitment to Christ and his Church, and in his dedication to service, especially to the poor and those most suffering.[23] A strong spiritual life and a realistic commitment to serve people converge in the continual transformation of the participant's mind and heart in harmony with Christ.

123.

Spiritual formation helps the participant to develop the ascetical tools that are necessary for spiritual growth, which include mortification, sacrifice, and generosity toward others. The participant must be open to conversion of heart about issues of justice, peace, and respect for life. He needs to be instructed regarding how his prayer, simplicity of life, and commitment to the poor add credibility to his capacity to witness to and, as a deacon, to preach effectively the Word of God.[24]

124.

Each person in formation is called to a mature relationship with those in authority, a relationship that includes a spirit of trust, mutual respect, and obedience. Accountability in formation is an invitation to a deeper conversion. A spirit of service to others is finally an imitation of Christ himself, who came to do not his own will but the will of his Father (Jn 5:30). Formation personnel, especially the spiritual director, should give instructions on the meaning of authentic obedience and help each participant to appreciate and practice it in his life.

125.

The role of the spiritual director, who must always be a priest,[25] is critical to the initial formation process, particularly in assisting the participant to discern and affirm the signs of his vocation.[26] An individual's spiritual director may be chosen directly by the participant, with the approval of the diocesan bishop, or from a list of spiritual directors similarly approved. The distinction between internal and external forums must always be clearly maintained. A participant may also consult (or be requested to do so) with an advisor whom he may select with the approval of the director of formation. The advisor, however, does not substitute for the unique role of the spiritual director in initial formation and discernment.[27]

126.

Participants should also be able to lead and engage others in prayer. This ministry of prayer with others is one of the most common activities of deacons as they visit homes, hospitals, prisons, engage in marriage preparation, and so on.

Intellectual Dimension

127.

Intellectual formation offers the participant "substantial nourishment" for the pastoral, human, and spiritual dimensions of his life. Intellectual formation is a "precious instrument" for effective discernment and ministry.[28] An increasingly educated society and the new roles of leadership in diaconal ministry require that a deacon be a knowledgeable and reliable witness to the faith and a spokesman for the Church's teaching. Therefore, the intellectual dimension of formation must be designed to communicate a knowledge of the faith and Church Tradition that is "complete and serious," so that each participant will be prepared to carry out his vital ministry.[29] "The commitment to study, which takes up no small part of the time of those preparing for the [diaconate] . . . is not in fact an external and secondary dimension of their human, Christian, spiritual and vocational growth. In reality, through study, especially the study of theology, the future [deacon] . . . assents to the word of God, grows in his spiritual life and prepares himself to fulfill his pastoral ministry."[30]

Intellectual Dimension Objectives

128.

Deacons must first understand and practice the essentials of Christian doctrine and life before they can communicate them to others in a clear way in their ministries of word, liturgy, and charity. Sacred Scripture is the soul of the program. Around it are structured the other branches of theology. Liturgical studies are to be given prominence, as the participants are prepared to lead the faith community in prayer and sacramental life. Preaching, with its preparation and practice, requires a significant segment of time in the program of study. Attention should also be given to topics reflecting the specific needs of the Church in the United States of America: (a) a family life perspective; (b) respect for and understanding of our national multicultural diversity and the incorporation of the Gospel into all aspects of society; (c) the social dimension of the Gospel as taught by the Church, especially in the social encyclicals of the popes; (d) an understanding of issues of particular concern for the Church in the United States of America and significant documents of the USCCB; and (e) the study of the beliefs and practices of other religions and Christian denominations—deepening a spirit of ecumenism and interreligious dialogue. Ample opportunities also need to be given for participants to study and practice missiology—learning how to evangelize—so as to form deacons who will be actively present in society, offering true diaconal witness, entering into sincere dialogue with others, and cooperating in charity to resolve common concerns.[31]

129.

The intellectual content should provide the participant with the knowledge, skills, and appreciation of the faith that he needs to effectively fulfill his ministry of Word, Liturgy, and charity. It should, therefore, be authentic and complete. In spite of the diversity of subjects, the intellectual dimension should offer an overall vision of faith that brings unity and harmony to the educational process.[32] The theological formation of the participants needs to be presented as originating from within the Church's life of faith, worship, and pastoral care.[33] In this way, intellectual formation will be perceived as crucial to the deacon's responsible exercise of his pastoral ministry.

130.

The intellectual dimension should also be constructed to help the participant "to evaluate his society and culture in light of the Gospel and to understand the Gospel in the light of the particular features of the society and culture in which he will be serving."[34] Of equal importance are the discernment and understanding of what is shared in common with other cultures and societies, as well as the cultural and ethnic expressions of the faith.

131.

Since participants enter formation as mature men, the intellectual dimension of formation "should make use of the methods and processes of adult education. . . . [The participants] should be invited to draw and reflect upon their adult life and faith experiences."[35]

132.

Theology is traditionally described as "faith seeking understanding." Therefore, the formation faculty and staff should structure an intellectual process that includes an invitation to each participant to reflect on his adult life and experience in the light of the Gospel and the

Church's teaching. The intellectual dimension in each stage of the formation program should be designed and presented in such a way as to integrate doctrine, morality, and spirituality.

133.

The following criteria focus the preparation and presentation of a systematic, comprehensive, and integrated intellectual formation, faithful to the Magisterium of the Church. This integrated intellectual formation is meant to support and prepare the deacon for his primary ministerial roles of word, liturgy, and charity.[36] Based on Scripture and Tradition, the documents of the Second Vatican Council, the *Catechism of the Catholic Church*, the *General Directory for Catechesis*,[37] and the *National Directory for Catechesis* of the USCCB, this formation must take into account the following theological and practical content:

a. Introduction to Sacred Scripture and its authentic interpretation; the theology of the Old and New Testaments; the interrelations among Scripture, Tradition, and the Magisterium; the use of Scripture in spiritual formation, preaching, evangelization, catechesis, and pastoral activity in general
b. Introduction to the study of the Fathers of the Church and an elementary knowledge of the history of the Church
c. Fundamental theology, with illustration of the sources; topics and methods of theology; presentation of the questions relating to Revelation and the formulation of the relationship between faith and reason, which will enable the participant to explain the reasonableness of the faith[38]
d. Dogmatic theology, with its various treatises: Trinity, creation, Christology, ecclesiology including the Church as a communion of Churches (Latin and Eastern Catholic Churches *sui iuris*),[39] ecumenism, Mariology, Christian anthropology, sacraments (especially theology of the ordained ministry), and eschatology
e. Christian morality in its personal, familial, and social dimensions, including the Church's teaching on sexuality, the social doctrine of the Church, and health care ethics
f. The USCCB's *Essential Norms for Diocesan/Eparchial Policies for Dealing with Allegations of Sexual Abuse of Minors by Priests or Deacons*

and *Charter for the Protection of Children and Young People*, as well as diocesan norms related to safe environment training

g. Spiritual theology, the spiritual traditions of the Church as applied to one's own spiritual journey, and the spiritual life of the faithful
h. Liturgy and its historical, spiritual, and juridical aspects, with particular attention to the Rite of Christian Initiation of Adults and to the liturgical rites the deacon will celebrate
i. Canon law, especially canonical considerations pertaining to rights and obligations, diocesan structures, preaching, sacraments and sacramentals, and the administration of temporal goods
j. Ecumenism and interreligious dialogue principles, norms, and dimensions in pastoral ministry[40]
k. Theology of Catholic evangelization: "evangelization of cultures and the inculturation of the message of faith," multicultural expressions of the faith, and missiology[41]

134.

This content is structured further in Norms 5 through 12 at the end of chapter six. Those responsible for the preparation of the academic component in the candidate and post-ordination stages of formation should determine a course of study that complies with this content prior to ordination, as well as a course of study that will further develop this content after ordination as part of a structured post-ordination program for continuing education and formation. Before ordination, the deacon candidate must demonstrate the proper level of competence in all these areas required for ordination and indicate his openness to further development by post-ordination continuing formation.

Pastoral Dimension

135.

An integral formation must relate the human, spiritual, and intellectual dimensions to pastoral practice. "The whole formation imparted to [the participants] . . . aims at preparing them to enter into communion with the charity of Christ. . . . Hence their formation in its different aspects must have a fundamentally pastoral character."[42] Within that context, the pastoral dimension in initial formation is not merely an apprenticeship to familiarize the participant in diaconal formation with some pastoral techniques. Its aim, however, is to initiate the participant into the sensitivity of what it means to be a disciple of Jesus, who came to serve and not to be served. Pastoral assignments embody this orientation, promoting learning through active engagement in a pastoral situation. Pastoral assignments foster a general integration in the formational process, forging a close link between the human, spiritual, and intellectual dimensions in formation. Evangelization; Catholic schools; catechetics; religious education; youth ministry; social justice outreach opportunities; rural ministry; ecumenism; prison ministry; the care of the sick, elderly, and dying; and service opportunities in varied cultural settings—all these indicate the breadth of experiences to which the participant may be exposed in the course of his pastoral formation.

Pastoral Dimension Objectives

136.

The pastoral dimension in diaconal formation should strengthen and enhance the exercise of the prophetic, priestly, and servant-leadership functions—deriving from his baptismal consecration—already lived and exercised by the participant in diaconal formation. In each stage of formation, he must be taught how to proclaim the Christian message and teach it, how to lead others in communal celebrations of liturgical prayer, and how to witness to the Church in a Christian service marked by charity. The demonstration of pastoral skills is a crucial element in the assessment of fitness for ordination. Therefore, the qualities to be developed for these tasks are as follows: a spirit of pastoral responsibility and servant-leadership, generosity and perseverance, ability to collaborate, creativity, respect for ecclesial communion, and filial obedience to the diocesan bishop. Through his participation in pastoral assignments, the participant should have a genuine confidence in his abilities and a realistic sense of his limitations.

137.

Initial pastoral formation should take into account that those preparing for the diaconate have already been involved in the mission of the Church.

The pastoral formation program should be designed, therefore, to build upon previous experiences and talents already displayed. In addition to identifying and developing the gifts already at work, the pastoral dimension of formation should aim at helping the participant to discover talents, perhaps unrecognized, and to develop the skills necessary for exercising the threefold diaconal ministry. A participant needs to demonstrate a genuine confidence in his own ability—a realistic sense of achieving the knowledge and skills required for an effective diaconal ministry—and a strong desire to serve in a broad range of ministerial circumstances.

138.

Pastoral formation interfaces with spiritual formation. It is a formation for an ever greater identification with the *diakonia* entrusted to the Church by Christ. Care is to be taken to introduce the participant actively into the pastoral life of the diocesan Church and to make a priority periodic meetings with the diocesan bishop, priests, other deacons, religious, and laity serving in official ministry, so as to ensure a coordinated unity for different pastoral activities.[43] Supervised pastoral formation placements should be designed and adapted to the needs of the individual participant, helping him to gradually and appropriately experience in his pastoral placement what he has learned in his study.[44] He should also be given ample opportunities to share experiences with deacons already in ministry.

139.

Pastoral formation develops by means of a specific theological discipline and a practical internship. This theological discipline, traditionally called pastoral theology, is "a scientific reflection on the Church as she is built up daily."[45] The pastoral dimension of formation needs to pay particular attention to the following elements:

a. **The Church's Ministry of the Word**—Proclamation of the Word in the varied contexts of ministerial service: *kerygma*, catechesis, homiletics (both in theory and practice), evangelization, and missiology[46]
b. **The Church's Ministry of Liturgy**—Liturgical praxis: celebration of the sacraments and sacramentals, service at the altar
c. **The Church's Ministry of Charity**—Educating and helping in the

exercise of the corporal and spiritual works of mercy by the Church; fostering by facilitation, motivation, and organization the Church's social justice ministry and the preferential option for the poor

140.

As part of his pastoral formation, the participant should acquire an appropriate multicultural awareness, exposure, and sensitivity, suitable to the needs of the diocese, including the possibility of learning a second language and studying its cultural context.[47]

141.

Other recommended elements for those in initial formation include the following:

a. Certain technical subjects that prepare the participant for specific pastoral care, such as pastoral counseling, with particular emphasis on appropriate referral, especially as applied to family ministry, catechetical pedagogy, sacred music, and ecclesiastical administration
b. A practical internship that permits the participant to encounter and respond in ministry to that which he has learned in his study
c. Progressive involvement in the pastoral activity of the diocese
d. An explanation of applicable norms and policies for marriage preparation and the canonical processes for declaring a marriage null
e. The developing of the participant's commitment to ecumenism and interreligious dialogue; appropriate shared pastoral experiences should be considered[48]
f. A maturing in the participant of "a strong missionary sensitivity"[49]
g. A commitment to the new evangelization[50]
h. An appropriate integration with other disciplines, such as philosophy, economics and politics, psychology, and sociology—according to particular situations and needs[51]
i. Information technology, distance learning, and the correct use of the Internet in pastoral ministry

142.

Pastoral formation must include theological reflection so the participant may integrate his ministerial activity with the broad scope of diaconal studies. This process should lead him to a lifelong effort in reflecting on his ministry in the light of faith.

III.
Additional Considerations

143.
Attention should be given to the following topics, which represent a value central to the life of the Catholic Church in the United States of America and, therefore, in the formation, ministry, and life of deacons.

A Family Life Perspective
Introduction

144.
A family life perspective is rooted in the challenge of St. John Paul II as stated in *Familiaris Consortio*: "No plan for organized pastoral work, at any level, must ever fail to take into consideration the pastoral care of the family."[52] Refocusing one's thinking from an individual-centered approach to a family-centered approach represents an important component in organizing diaconal formation, ministry, and life.

145.
To assist the director of formation and the Director of the Permanent Diaconate in complying with this injunction while preparing and implementing a diocesan plan, organization, and schedule for the formation, ministry, and life of deacons, *A Family Perspective in Church and Society*, published by the USCCB Committee on Marriage and Family, will prove useful.[53] In reflecting upon the experience of the Synod of Bishops convoked in 1980 by St. John Paul II on the topic of family life in the modern world, as well as his 1981 apostolic exhortation *On the Family* (*Familiaris Consortio*), the committee authored this document with the intent "to elicit continuing pastoral action in support of family life." The entire document needs to be read, studied, and reflected upon "so that the concept of a family perspective will have practical implications" in the formation, ministry, and life of deacons.[54]

More recently, Pope Francis, in his apostolic exhortation *Amoris Laetitia*, outlines additional aspects of accompanying couples through the challenges of married life.[55]

In light of all of the above resources, those responsible for formation need to do the following:

a. "Keep up-to-date with family changes and trends in the nation and in their locale, and then examine their policies, programs, ministries, and service in light of this information."
b. "Be sensitive to the fact that many kinds of families participate" in the various church programs in which deacons minister.
c. "Be sensitive to the special needs families experience and the pressures and stress these needs create. Leaders need to help families identify these pressures, and in partnership help families deal with them."
d. "Be sensitive, in planning, to the time and energy commitments of families where both parents—or the only parent—are employed."
e. "Be sensitive to the economic pressures families experience today."
f. "Understand that all programs affect families, even programs aimed at individuals. All social institutions, including the Church, make a direct or indirect impact on the unity, well-being, health, and stability of families. There is a tendency to replace family responsibilities, in part or in their entirety, by social institutions or to marginalize families' participation in the various programs and services provided by these institutions because these services are designed primarily for individuals."
g. "Help families manage their coordinating and mediating responsibility, rather than complicate it. For example, parish leaders often tell family members that their participation in parish programs is imperative. But families need to be active participants in determining parish priorities, and they have a responsibility to determine their participation . . . based on a realistic assessment of their energy, family time, and resources."
h. Recognize that "what the Church does and how it does it [together] affect the unity, well-being, health, and stability of families. Church leaders need to be more aware of how the Church's policies, programs, ministries, and services can either help or hinder families in

fulfilling their own basic responsibilities. Church leaders need to see themselves as partners with families."[56]

146.

Individuals do not enter into formation alone. Those who participate in diaconal formation, married or unmarried, come with their families. They come as members of a family, known as the "domestic Church," where life is shared and nurtured. They come from that primary community, where God is first discovered and known, and enter into a new and wider community that can expand their love and deepen their faith. They come with their experiences of faith and personal life.

147.

Each participant must explore ways to keep his family life as a priority in the face of the growing demands of formation and ministry, which include issues of age, faith, health, economics, employment, and relationships.

The Married Participant

148.

In deciding to pursue a possible diaconal vocation, a married man must comply with the wishes of his wife, in a spirit of mutual commitment and love. A wife is an equal partner in the Sacrament of Matrimony and is an individual person with her own gifts, talents, and call from God. A man's diaconal formation can be a unique and challenging situation and opportunity for his wife. She should be involved in the program in appropriate ways—remembering, however, that it is the husband who is responding to a call to the diaconate. The Church has determined that a married man cannot be considered for the diaconate without the consent of his wife.[57] The consent offered by way of a wife's signature should be reflective of her participation and presence at some level. Otherwise, it cannot be an informed consent. After ordination, a deacon's wife needs to "be duly informed of [her] husband's activities in order to arrive at a harmonious balance between family, professional and ecclesial responsibilities."[58]

149.

The participation of a wife in her husband's formation program strengthens their awareness of the husband's diaconal vocation and helps the wife to accept the challenges and changes that will take place, should her husband be ordained. It also provides an opportunity for those responsible for diaconal formation to assess whether she has "the Christian moral character and attributes which will neither hinder [her] husband's ministry nor be out of keeping with it."[59] To help the participant's wife to give an informed consent to her husband's request for ordination, it is necessary to include appropriate resources and programming addressed to her. Spiritual direction may be made available to her while her husband is in formation. When workshops and spiritual exercises for wives are planned, wives should be consulted to ascertain their questions and concerns. While every effort ought to be made to provide scheduling and material assistance to make wives' participation possible, care must simultaneously be taken to keep clear the essential distinction between ordained and familial life and the clear independence of diaconal ministry.[60] The level of expected participation of the wife in the formation process should consider her responsibilities to family and work. Care also should be extended to those who are recently widowed—normally, at least three years should elapse prior to acceptance. Those recently married should live their married vocation for five years prior to requesting admittance.

150.

Given that the married deacon should be a model for Christian family life, careful examination of a participant's marital history is essential. Men who are in an irregular marriage and have not yet approached a marriage tribunal, or men who are discovered to be in a marriage celebrated without canonical form which has not yet been convalidated, cannot be considered for a diaconal formation program until their marital status is regularized in the Church. Men who have been civilly divorced must receive a declaration of nullity prior to entry into a diaconal formation program. Any irregularities need to be resolved prior to entry into a formation program. The circumstances surrounding those men who have entered into more than one marriage or who first entered into civil unions only later recognized by the Church require the exercise of great caution. In the latter cases, the participant's attitude toward church teaching on marriage needs scrutiny. The same caution applies to applicants who have received a declaration of matrimonial nullity; such men should be carefully screened. It is important to ascertain whether and how previous obstacles to a marriage commitment or possible scandal might affect their viability as participants for the permanent diaconate. Care must be taken to ascertain the canonical declaration of nullity by reviewing the relevant documentation to ensure that the reasons and circumstances that serve as warrants for the declaration of nullity are fully disclosed to the diocesan bishop. All such cases should be carefully weighed.

151.

Children of participants also need to be included in the formation process in "appropriate ways."[61] This will depend, among other considerations, on their ages, circumstances, and interests. These occasions provide opportunities for parents and their children to support and assist each other in keeping communication open and expectations clear. Younger children and teens especially need to be encouraged to express their concerns about the public role of this ministry and how it affects their lives both within the family and among their peers. They need to express honestly their concerns over the commitment of time and energy by their parents and what this means to the life of the family and to each member. This is not only a family concern; it is a formation concern.

152.

A man's diaconal formation can be a gift in the life of his family, providing it with an opportunity to explore together the meaning of discipleship, the Church, and the vocations of marriage and Holy Orders. It can strengthen the bonds between parents and their children through prayer, communication, and shared virtue. It can also be a powerful experience of community, service, and compassion.

The Unmarried Participant

153.

What has been described regarding the role of the family in the formation of a married man also applies to the family of the unmarried participant (i.e., one who never married, one now widowed, or one civilly divorced[62]). His family should likewise be invited to share appropriately in the formation community. His parents and siblings, any children, and extended family need similar grounding in understanding the ministry of the deacon so they can be supportive and encouraging of his vocation. The unmarried participant must likewise demonstrate that he is able to fulfill his responsibilities for the care of any minor children or other dependents.

154.

The unmarried participant must grow in clear and realistic understanding of the value of celibate chastity and its connection to diaconal ministry.[63] To be lived fruitfully, the value of celibacy must be internalized. To achieve these formation goals, the unmarried participant should be incorporated into a mentoring group composed of priests and celibate deacons from whom he can receive support and encouragement, a group where a dialogue on the challenges and a faith-filled response to a celibate lifestyle can be fostered.

Multicultural Diversity

155.

Deacons are called to serve a multiracial, multiethnic, multicultural Church. This changing face of the Catholic Church in the United States of America has a significant effect on diaconal formation. The cultures and traditions of those in diaconal formation—mirroring as they do the rich diversity of gifts and unity in faith—need to be respected, valued, and understood. Formation must be sensitive and responsive to the circumstances of different cultures,[64] especially in their unique patterns of learning and of expressing their understanding. There should be formal instruction regarding the developmental role and function of culture in the life of the individual and community. Recognizing the cultural diversity of the Catholic Church in the United States of America and incorporating experiences and an appreciation of it all enhance the present and future ministerial effectiveness of each participant.

156.

Formation objectives and methods should accommodate an appropriate inculturation of each participant to foster his effective service within a multicultural community. Given the ethnic and racial diversity of our national population and the mobility that is so characteristic of our society, a participant in diaconal formation ought to have meaningful cross-cultural experiences and specific training for ministry in his own cultural context. This would include reasonable levels of language study in areas where large numbers of Catholics are not proficient in English. As an ordained servant-leader in a Church called to welcome and embrace all people, the deacon should be a living example of that spirit, one who is particularly conscious of the potential for misunderstanding and alienation that can occur when cultural, ethnic, or racial diversity becomes an occasion of discrimination rather than of social harmony.[65]

Social Justice

157.

The ministry of charity is "most characteristic of the deacon."[66] "In fact, with sacred ordination, [the deacon] is constituted a living icon of Christ the servant within the Church."[67] From its beginnings, the ministry of the deacon encompassed stewardship of the Church's material goods, making evident the claim of the poor on the resources of the community. Deacons have long helped to ensure that the allocation of those resources made provision for meaningful assistance to those who suffered from poverty, hunger, homelessness, and disease. Today, the restored diaconate maintains this traditional stewardship through its commitment to the poor.

158.

Diaconal formation should equip deacons for working on behalf of the poor and indeed for working to put into effect the full range of the social teaching of the Church. Formation programs should help the participant to grow in an understanding of the Church's teaching and tradition of social justice. Deacons should become familiar with the social encyclicals of the popes and the relevant documents issued by the USCCB on matters such as the integrity of human life from conception to death, the economy, racism, immigration, and peace. Formation programs should impart the skills needed to promote Catholic social teaching in the marketplace, parish, and diocese.

A Spirit of Ecumenism and Interreligious Dialogue

159.

The Second Vatican Council taught that the restoration of full visible communion among all Christians is the will of Christ and is essential to the life of the Catholic Church.[68] An ecumenical spirit should be integrated into all aspects of formation. Those who are or will be engaged in pastoral ministry must acquire "an authentically ecumenical disposition"[69] in their lives and ministry. The purpose of formation in ecumenism is to educate hearts and minds in the necessary human and religious dispositions that favor the search for Christian unity. A genuine ecumenism should be thoroughly incorporated into all aspects of diaconal formation,[70] remembering that "genuine ecumenical formation must not remain solely academic; it should also include ecumenical experience."[71]

160.

The Second Vatican Council also urged "its sons and daughters to enter with prudence and charity into discussion and collaboration with members of other religions."[72] Such a spirit must imbue a desire for ecumenical and interreligious cooperation with Jews, Muslims, and members of other religions. The formation program must assist the participant in achieving a spirit of welcome, respect, and collaboration among people of good will. "The world, looking to us believers, exhorts us to cooperate amongst ourselves and with the men and women of good will who profess no religion, asking us for effective responses regarding numerous issues: peace, hunger, the poverty that afflicts millions of people, the environmental crisis, violence, especially that committed in the name of religion, corruption, moral decay, the crisis of the family, of the economy, of finance, and especially of hope."[73] The deacon may serve to link the Catholic Church to other Christian communities, other faith traditions, and civic organizations to address pressing social needs and to foster a collaborative sharing of material resources and personnel in response to those needs.[74] Diaconal formation should model and facilitate this collaborative cooperation.

IV.
Assessment: Integrating the Four Dimensions in Formation Programming

161.

"To each individual the manifestation of the Spirit is given for some benefit" (1 Cor 12:7). All ministry flows out of the gifts of the Holy Spirit. These gifts are given to the People of God not for the benefit of the individual minister but for the benefit of the Church. As a result, any discernment of gifts and charisms must involve the ecclesial community. Since the charisms are ecclesial, any discernment process must also be ecclesial in nature. This is especially true for the ordained ministries of the Church. An individual who presents himself for ordination to the diaconate is accountable to the Church, who discerns—confirms—his vocation.

162.

It is essential, therefore, that those who are responsible for selection and initial formation, including pastoral placement, discern whether the participant has integrated the various dimensions in formation that are needed for an effective diaconal ministry. Further, consultation with the participant's pastor, the faculty, other pastoral assignment supervisors, mentors, those whom the participant serves, and, if married, his wife is crucial to the discernment process. The surest indicator, however, is the participant's previous and present effectiveness in Church service.

163.

If conducted seriously and communicated frankly, assessments can be valuable occasions for the discernment, affirmation, and development of a vocation. Assessments should be made and communicated on a regular basis. There are multiple ways of assessing, including self-assessment, formation team and mentor assessment, and peer and pastoral supervisory assessment, to name but a few. Different situations require different forms and levels of assessment. However, a succinct annual self-assessment written by the participant based on the four dimensions of formation is a valuable tool for the Church and for the participant as his vocation is discerned; an annual self-assessment should be considered as an element of the formation program.

164.

Every assessment, however, has a dual purpose. It affirms the participant in identifying his gifts and capabilities, exhibits areas for his further growth and development, and indicates his limitations. It concurrently provides a similar assessment of the formation program itself. The assessment outcome of an individual participant can demonstrate the program's achievement in integrating the various dimensions of formation, that is, the effectiveness of its structures and scheduling, and the competency of its formators, professors, staff, and administrators. Simply stated, the assessment of the individual participant also points out the strength, potential, and limitation of the initial formation program.

165.

The following are some indicators that an initial formation program is successful, measured by the participant's ability to manifest:

a. An increase in holiness of life
b. An ability to clearly articulate the Catholic faith
c. The capacity to apply church teaching and practice to concrete societal issues and pastoral concerns
d. A sensitivity to enculturate the Gospel within the communities in which he lives, works, and ministers

e. His embrace of the universal nature of the Church and its missionary evangelical spirit
f. A balanced capacity for and commitment to the ministries of word, liturgy, and charity, demonstrated in his words and deeds
g. A commitment to ongoing growth in the human, spiritual, intellectual, and pastoral dimensions of formation
h. A capacity to foster the communion and mission of the lay faithful, in collaboration with the diocesan bishop and presbyterate
i. An obedient and humble service to all in the name of the Church
j. His ability to celebrate, in accordance with the Church's legislation and with due reverence and devotion, those liturgical and sacramental acts that the Church entrusts to the deacon

166.

All stages, both initial and ongoing, of a well-conceived diocesan formation program will comply fully with the Congregation for Catholic Education's document *Basic Norms for the Formation of Permanent Deacons*, as well as this *National Directory*.

Norms

1. Three separate but integral stages constitute a unified diocesan formation program for deacons: aspirant, candidate, and post-ordination. (112)
2. Each stage should include the four dimensions for a complete formation process: human, spiritual, intellectual, and pastoral. (112)
3. The role of the spiritual director, who must always be a priest, is critical to the formation process, particularly in assisting the participant in discerning and affirming the signs of his vocation. (125)
4. Intellectual formation must introduce the diaconal participant and the ordained deacon to the fundamental teachings of the Church covering the areas delineated by the document *Basic Norms for the Formation of Permanent Deacons*, as well as by this *National Directory*. It is essential that before ordination the participant have a thorough knowledge of the Catholic faith and be able to communicate it effectively. (133)

5. During formation, the participant should have ample opportunities to participate appropriately in pastoral experience. (139-141)
6. Pastoral formation must include theological reflection so the participant may integrate his ministerial activity with the broad scope of diaconal studies. (142)
7. A married man cannot be considered for the diaconate without the consent of his wife. (148)
8. While every effort ought to be made to involve the wife of a married participant and deacon in an appropriate level of participation in her husband's formation, care must simultaneously be taken to keep clear the essential distinction between ordained and familial life and the clear independence of diaconal ministry. (149)
9. The cultures and traditions of those in diaconal formation—mirroring as they do the rich diversity of gifts in the Church—need to be respected and valued. Formation, therefore, must be sensitive and adapted to the circumstances of different cultures. (155)
10. Assessments are valuable occasions for the discernment, affirmation, and development of a participant's vocation. Assessments should be made and communicated on a regular basis. (163)
11. All stages, both initial and ongoing, of a well-conceived diocesan formation program will comply fully with the document of the Congregation for Catholic Education *Basic Norms for the Formation of Permanent Deacons*, as well as this *National Directory*. (166)

---

[1] PDV, no. 42.

[2] BNFPD, nos. 66-88.

[3] PDV, no. 43.

[4] Second Vatican Council, *Decree on the Apostolate of Lay People (Apostolicam Actuositatem) (November 18, 1965), no. 2, www.vatican.va/archive/hist_councils/ii_vatican_council/documents/vat-ii_decree_19651118_apostolicam-actuositatem_en.html.*

[5] "Ordination of a Deacon," chap. 2 of *Ordination of Deacons, Priests, and Bishops*, in The Rites of the Catholic Church, vol. 2 (Collegeville, MN: Liturgical Press, 1991), no. 14.

[6] GDC, nos. 222-223.

[7] Congregation for the Evangelization of Peoples, *Guide for Catechists* (December 3, 1993) (Washington, DC: United States Catholic Conference, 1993), no. 21, emphasis original.

[8] BNFPD, nos. 66-70.

[9] BNFPD, no. 67.

[10] BNFPD, no. 68.

[11] BNFPD, no. 69; see PDV, no. 44.

[12] BNFPD, no. 66, citing PDV, no. 43.

[13] BNFPD, no. 66.

[14] BNFPD, no. 71.

[15] Pope Benedict XVI, Encyclical *God Is Love* (*Deus Caritas Est*) (Washington, DC: USCCB, 2006), no. 1.

[16] BNFPD, nos. 32-33.

[17] These demonstrations of maturity presuppose that he is already meeting his obligations to attend weekly Sunday Mass and all Holy Days of Obligation. "On Sundays and other holy days of obligation, the faithful are obliged to participate in the Mass." CIC, c. 1247.

[18] BNFPD, no. 71.

[19] BNFPD, no. 72.

[20] BNFPD, no. 73.

[21] PDV, nos. 47-49.

[22] DMLPD, nos. 50-62. See BNFPD, no. 12.

[23] BNFPD, no. 11.

[24] BNFPD, no. 72. See PDV, no. 30.

[25] BNFPD, no. 23.

[26] BNFPD, nos. 1, 2.

[27] BNFPD, nos. 70, 76. See PDV, no. 66.

[28] BNFPD, no. 79.

[29] BNFPD, no. 79.

[30] PDV, no. 51.

[31] PDV, nos. 51-56.

[32] BNFPD, no. 85.

[33] PDV, no. 53.

[34] PDG (1984), no. 76.

[35] PDG (1984), no. 77.

[36] See ADUS.

[37] GDC, no. 120.

[38] See St. John Paul II, Encyclical *On the Relationship Between Faith and Reason* (*Fides et Ratio*) (Washington, DC: United States Catholic Conference, 1998).

[39] Committee on the Relationship between Eastern and Latin Catholic Churches, NCCB, *Eastern Catholics in the United States of America* (Washington, DC: United States Catholic Conference, 1999).

[40] Pontifical Council for Promoting Christian Unity, *The Ecumenical Dimension in the Formation of Pastoral Workers* (March 9, 1998), *in Ecumenical Formation of Pastoral Workers* (Washington, DC: United States Catholic Conference, 1998). See BNFPD, no. 88.

[41] PDV, no. 55.

[42] PDV, no. 57; see BNFPD, no. 85.

[43] DMLPD, no. 78.

[44] BNFPD, no. 87.

[45] PDV, no. 57.

[46] See EG, nos. 135-159; Congregation for Divine Worship and the Discipline of the Sacraments, *Homiletic Directory* (Washington, DC: USCCB, 2015); and USCCB, *Preaching the Mystery of Faith: The Sunday Homily* (Washington, DC: USCCB, 2013). One may not speak during the homily time of Mass unless he is an ordained priest or deacon. *General Instruction on the Roman Missal*, no. 66; Congregation for Divine Worship and the Discipline of the Sacraments, Instruction *Redemptionis Sacramentum* (2004), no. 161; CIC, cc. 766, 767 §1; *Sunday Celebrations in the Absence of a Priest* (Washington, DC: USCCB, 2007), no. 43; Congregation for the Clergy et al., *Instruction on Certain Questions Regarding the Collaboration of the Non-Ordained Faithful in the Sacred Ministry of Priest* (August 15, 1997), art. 3 §1, *www.vatican.va/roman_curia/pontifical_councils/laity/documents/rc_con_interdic_doc_15081997_en.html*; and complementary legislation from the United States Conference of Catholic Bishops, "Canon 766—Lay Preaching," *www.usccb.org/beliefs-and-teachings/what-we-believe/canon-law/complementary-norms/canon-766-lay-preaching*.

[47] See Committee on Cultural Diversity in the Church, USCCB, *Building Intercultural Competence for Ministers* (Washington, DC: USCCB, 2012).

[48] Pontifical Council for Promoting Christian Unity, *Ecumenical Dimension*.

[49] BNFPD, no. 88.

[50] "The joy of the gospel fills the hearts and lives of all who encounter Jesus. Those who accept his offer of salvation are set free from sin, sorrow, inner emptiness and loneliness. With Christ joy is constantly born anew. . . . I wish to encourage the Christian faithful to embark upon a new chapter of evangelization marked by this joy." EG, no. 1.

[51] BNFPD, nos. 81, 86.

[52] St. John Paul II, Apostolic Exhortation *On the Family* (*Familiaris Consortio*) (Washington, DC: United States Catholic Conference, 1981), no. 70.

[53] Committee on Marriage and Family, USCCB, *A Family Perspective in Church and Society*, 10th anniversary ed. (Washington, DC: USCCB, 1998).

[54] Committee on Marriage and Family, *Family Perspective in Church and Society*, v, vi.

[55] Pope Francis, Post-Synodal Apostolic Exhortation *The Joy of Love* (*Amoris Laetitia*) (Washington, DC: USCCB, 2016), nos. 223-230.

[56] FP, 10-11, 46-47. See DMLPD, no. 61; BNFPD, no. 27.

[57] CIC, c. 1031 §2. See BNFPD, no. 37.

[58] DMLPD, no. 61.

[59] BNFPD, no. 37.

[60] DMLPD, no. 81.

[61] BNFPD, no. 56; see DMLPD, nos. 61, 81.

[62] "While the decision to accept such a [divorced] man remains with the bishop, it must be exercised with the highest caution and prudence. This is particularly so if the candidate has had his marriage declared null by a Church tribunal on psychological grounds (see Letter of the Sacred Congregation for Catholic Education, July 8, 1983, Prot. N. 657/83 & 982/80/136, to His Excellency the Most Rev. John Roach, Archbishop of St. Paul and Minneapolis, President of the Episcopal Conference of the USA, concerning the admission to seminary of men whose marriages have been declared null by ecclesiastical tribunals)." Congregation for Catholic Education and the Congregation for the Clergy, *Joint Study of the US Draft Document–The National Directory for the Formation, Ministry and Life of Permanent Deacons in the United States*, Prot. No. 78/2000 (March 4, 2002).

[63] PDV, no. 29.

[64] BNFPD, no. 10.

[65] Bishops' Committee on Migration, NCCB, *One Family Under God*, rev. ed. (Washington, DC: United States Catholic Conference, 1998), 20.

[66] BNFPD, no. 9.

[67] BNFPD, no. 11.

[68] See Second Vatican Council, *Decree on Ecumenism* (*Unitatis Redintegratio*) (Washington, DC: United States Catholic Conference, 1964), nos. 1-4.

[69] Pontifical Council for Promoting Christian Unity, *Directory for the Application of Principles and Norms on Ecumenism* (March 25, 1993), no. 70.

[70] Pontifical Council for Promoting Christian Unity, *Ecumenical Dimension*, nos. 2-4. See also nos. 16-29.

[71] Pontifical Council for Promoting Christian Unity, *Ecumenical Dimension*, no. 28.

[72] Second Vatican Council, *Declaration on the Relation of the Church to Non-Christian Religions* (Nostra Aetate) (Washington, DC: United States Catholic Conference, 1965), no. 2.

[73] Pope Francis, Interreligious General Audience on the Occasion of the Fiftieth Anniversary of *Nostra Aetate* (October 28, 2015), www.vatican.va/content/francesco/en/audiences/2015/documents/papa-francesco_20151028_udienza-generale.html.

[74] Pontifical Council for Promoting Christian Unity, *Ecumenical Dimension*. See Pontifical Council for Promoting Christian Unity, *Ecumenical Formation: Ecumenical Reflections and Suggestions* (May 20, 1993), III, nos. 17-25, in *Ecumenical Formation of Pastoral Workers* (Washington, DC: United States Catholic Conference, 1998).

Chapter Four

Vocation, Discernment, and Selection

I.
Promotion and Recruitment

167.

THE FIRST LETTER OF ST. PAUL TO TIMOTHY provides the first principle for the selection of deacons: "They should be tested first; then, if there is nothing against them, let them serve as deacons" (3:10). Those who have worked closely with the reestablishment of the diaconate conclude that the diaconate is a particular vocation called forth by the Holy Spirit, that a successful process of training and development can only cooperate with and build upon fundamental preexisting traits and dispositions that point to a diaconal vocation, and that the process of training and development can be successful only in supportive life circumstances. Such life circumstances include but are not limited to a stable marriage (if the candidate is married), a stable family life, and a career that does not violate Church teaching or canon law and allows sufficient time and energy for formation.

168.

The promotion and recruitment of qualified men for the diaconate should be a collaborative ministry between the staffs of the diocesan vocations office and the diaconate office, as well as the diocesan bishop and pastors. The diaconate office should communicate with the vocations office and other diocesan entities to promote the awareness of diaconal vocations and ways to pursue a vocation to the diaconate. If a man has been dismissed from the seminary or another diaconal formation program, additional care should be taken, including a thorough investigation into the reason for dismissal, prior to admitting him into the diaconal formation program. If the diocesan Church wishes to nominate appropriate men, it may be helpful for the diocesan diaconate office to prepare guidelines, approved by the diocesan bishop, that provide specific information about recruitment, as well as the selection and formation processes. If there is a diocesan pastoral plan for ministry in which deacons have an important role, then the diocese and parishes can more easily identify and recruit potential candidates, describe to them the challenges and opportunities of diaconal ministry in the diocese, and urge them to consider it as a service to which they can commit themselves.

169.

The Church in the United States of America is enriched by the diversity of its cultural, racial, and ethnic communities. Because these communities share in the responsibility for promoting church vocations, their leaders ought to be formally invited and included in the planning and implementation of vocation programs directed to their communities. Their support and encouragement will effectively assist in the recruitment of qualified applicants from their communities. Representatives of US ethnic and cultural communities—such as Americans of African, Pacific Islander, Asian, Native American, and Hispanic heritage—who participate as consultants to the diaconate office can provide significant insight on cultural subtleties and their effect upon discernment and formation programming, including pastoral placement.

170.

Of particular importance in the United States of America is the large Hispanic Catholic population. Knowledge of Spanish and of Hispanic cultures is important in both recruiting and retaining Hispanic candidates. In each stage of formation, essential resources—e.g., translators, textbooks, mentors, community support—should be provided to ensure the inclusion of each participant.

171.

Care ought to be taken, especially in the post-ordination stage of formation, to provide opportunities for English-speaking deacons to learn Spanish, or other appropriate languages used in the diocese, on a conversational level. The opportunity for formal study of Hispanic and other cultures also should be provided. Further, the study of English and the historical development of a multicultural society within the United States of America should be provided to those whose primary language is not English.

172.

The above discussion regarding the recruitment and retention of Hispanic candidates applies to each cultural, racial, and ethnic community, especially Native American communities. Those responsible for recruitment, discernment, and formation have a responsibility to exercise multicultural sensitivity. They need to appreciate cultural subtleties and differences, acknowledging the historical constrictions experienced within these communities. Further, familiarity with family structures and traditions is important. This cultural/racial/ethnic orientation and sensitivity enables recruiters and those involved in formation to competently discern and foster diaconal vocations within these diverse communities.

II.
The Mystery of Vocation

173.

"The history . . . of every Christian vocation, is the history of an *inexpressible dialogue between God and human beings*, between the love of God who calls and the freedom of individuals who respond lovingly to him."[1] This calling-forth from God is marked first in the reception of the Sacraments of Christian Initiation. Then from out of this body of believers, Christ calls some of his disciples to service for the whole Church. The Church discerns this calling and, if it is found worthy, asks the diocesan bishop to ordain them to Holy Orders.

174.

From the experience of the restored diaconate in the United States of America, certain behavioral patterns have been discerned among exemplary deacons: a "natural inclination of service to the . . . Christian community"[2] and to all in need; psychological integrity; a capacity for dialogue, which implies a sense of docility and openness; the ability to share one's faith yet listen respectfully to other points of view; the capacity to listen carefully and without prejudices—respecting people in the context of their religion, race, gender, ethnicity, and culture; good communication skills; a sense of responsibility that includes fulfilling one's word and completing one's work; self-directed and collaborative accountability; balanced and prudent judgment; generosity in service; and the ability to lead, motivate, facilitate, and animate others into appropriate action and service.[3]

175.

The profile is completed with certain spiritual and evangelical qualities. Among these are a sound faith; good Christian reputation; active involvement in the Church's apostolate; personal integrity, maturity, and holiness; regular participation in the Church's sacramental life; evidence of recognized, ongoing commitment to the Church's life and service; participation in faith enrichment opportunities (e.g., retreats, days of recollection, adult education programming); a stable marriage, if married, or a mature celibate state of life, if single; active membership in a Christian community; capacity for obedience and fraternal communion; and a deep spirituality and prayer life. The presence of these qualities, experienced in kindness and humility, may demonstrate a call to the Order of Deacons.[4]

176.

Additional considerations that need to be stressed are the element of readiness and the timeliness of one's response to a vocation. Since inquirers to the diaconate have many commitments to family, career, employment, community, and church service, it is a matter of prudential judgment to explore not only whether the call to the diaconate comes from the Holy Spirit, but also whether the inquirer is ready and able to respond to that call at the present time.

III.
The Discernment of the Call

177.

The first stirrings of a vocation to the diaconate are often explored at a personal level and usually begin with seeking information about the diaconate and formation. Here, an individual initially reflects upon the nature of his perceived call. Primacy must be given at this time to the spiritual dimension, and central to this is spiritual guidance. Pope Francis refers to the "art of accompaniment" as steady and reassuring, encouraging growth in the Christian life.[5] The individual's pastor and others on the parish staff are particular resources at this time.

178.

Because the majority of those who inquire about the diaconate are married, they should be directed to pay particular attention to discussing their possible vocation with their wives and families. The initial information and conversations with their pastor and others should assist and encourage these discussions. For a married man, the support and consent of his wife is required. Therefore, both spouses need to make sure that support and consent, even at this early stage of discernment, arise from an informed understanding. Careful consideration must be given in those rare cases where an applicant to the diaconal formation program is in a mixed marriage or a disparity of cult marriage. If the applicant is accepted into the program, this situation may require additional preparation for the participant and his wife. Many regions and cultures also place emphasis on the participation of the extended family. This, too, is an important resource for discernment.

179.

An inquiry and eventual application for entrance into diaconal formation constitute not just a personal and family journey. The Church must accompany it. The parish is the primary experience of Church for most inquirers. It is the responsibility of this community and, in particular, its pastor to invite from among its members those who may be qualified to serve as ordained ministers of the Church.[6] Similarly, those church and community agencies that have often carried out the Church's mission of charity and social justice have a unique opportunity to call forth appropriate nominees from among their personnel.

180.

An inquiry about the diaconate and the formation process eventually includes the diocesan Church. Information sessions, the exploration of the criteria for a diaconal vocation, and particular counsel presented by the diocesan diaconate office can aid an individual in his decision to move forward to a formal application.

181.

When the inquirer is presented to the diocese by his pastor and submits an application, the formal process for admission begins. This initial discernment continues with particular focus on the applicant's abilities and potential for ordained ministry. Both the applicant and the diocesan Church enter into an intensive screening process.

IV.
Admission and Selection Procedures

The Role of the Pastor and Parish Community

182.

The inquirer who seeks consideration for ordination to the diaconate needs to enter into dialogue with his parish community. It is the pastor who initially presents him for consideration into diaconal formation through a letter that confirms he is a practicing Catholic of good repute and in good standing.[7] This letter should attest that the man shows evidence of the qualities, attitudes, experience, and spirituality deemed necessary for admission into formation, namely:

a. He is actively involved in parish and other community service.
b. He is in full communion with the Church. (At least five years should elapse between a convert's or returning Catholic's entry into the Church and his acceptance into formation; care must be given to

someone in whom a sudden conversion experience seems to precipitate a diaconal vocation.)

c. He is in a stable marriage, if married, or in a mature celibate state of life, if single.
d. If married, he has the consent of his wife.
e. He is properly motivated and gives evidence of an overall personal balance and moral character.
f. He is a frequent participant in adult faith enrichment opportunities (e.g., retreats, days of reflection, spiritual direction, study of Scripture and church teachings).
g. He is free of canonical impediments or irregularities.[8]

The Role of the Diocese

183.

The director of formation, who coordinates the selection process, arranges an interview with the diocese's committee on admission.[9] The purpose of the interview is to assess the applicant's level of awareness of a diaconal vocation, as well as to obtain information and background on his family life, employment stability, and general aptitude for diaconal ministry. The interview must include a separate interview with his wife, if he is married, and may include an interview with the entire family.

184.

As part of the application process, those charged with admission must—with appropriate care for confidentiality and manifestation of conscience—explore the presence of impediments to ordination.[10] If canonical dispensations are required, these must be obtained before admission to aspirant formation.

185.

Appropriate psychological consultation must be included as part of the application process, but always with the explicit, free, informed, and written consent of the applicant.[11] Those selected as psychological consultants must use psychological methods in harmony with Christian anthropology and Catholic teaching, particularly with respect to the theology of the diaconal vocation, the various states of life of the deacon, and the basic human qualities expected of a mature deacon. They also should obtain any pertinent and helpful information received in the admission process regarding the applicant. Care also must be taken in the selection of psychological consultants who will be assigned to applicants whose primary language is not English. A marriage indicator may be included for married applicants. Results from the chosen indicator should be reviewed by admissions personnel prior to any admissions decision.

Required Application Documents

186.

Required application documents include the following:

a. A church certificate of Baptism, Confirmation, and, if relevant, Matrimony, issued within the preceding six months[12]
b. Proof of age (in accord with canon law,[13] the USCCB has established the minimum age of ordination at thirty-five years)
c. A completed application form and, as appropriate, a consent form regarding psychological consultation and the confidentiality of consultative reports[14]
d. A recent photograph of the nominee[15] and, if married, of his wife, for administrative and faculty identification
e. A personal handwritten statement from the wife of a married applicant indicating her initial consent for his application and entrance into aspirant formation[16]
f. Letters of recommendation[17]
g. Results from a recent physical examination to ensure that applicants possess the good health necessary for diaconal formation and ministry (this exam should include HIV and drug testing)
h. An official transcript of past or present academic studies[18]
i. "A written report of the rector of any previous house in which the candidate has spent time in formation,"[19] including "explicit reference to the evaluations of the candidate and the votes he received"[20]
j. A written report from the director of any previous diaconal formation

program in which the applicant has spent time in formation, including explicit reference to the evaluations of the applicant and the votes he received

k. A thorough criminal, cyber, and social media profile background check of each nominee under the auspices of the diocesan diaconate office, including a report of the applicant's financial stability
l. Proof of legal residency and canonical domicile or quasi-domicile in the diocese[21]
m. A letter of recommendation from the applicant's employer[22]
n. A personal autobiography, which is helpful in getting to know the applicant more intimately

Discernment of Readiness for the Aspirant Stage of Formation

187.

Assessment of readiness at the application level is accomplished in a variety of ways. Common resources are letters of recommendation by those who know the applicant; a self-assessment prepared by the applicant, usually as an autobiographical statement; an interview with the committee on admission, and a review of his pastoral experience, especially noting any experience with the poor and the marginalized. Intellectual readiness is often assessed on the basis of prior experience through academic transcripts from schools attended and through evidence of participation in a lay ecclesial ministry formation program, parish adult education programs, or similar adult religious training.

V.
Admission into the Aspirant Stage of Formation

188.

The diocese's committee on admission must develop a procedural process to review the application dossier of each applicant. Because admission into the initial stages of formation occurs through two distinct but unified processes—(1) acceptance into the aspirant stage; (2) admittance into the candidate stage of diaconal formation[23]—the committee should nominate to the diocesan bishop only those applicants whom they have judged as possessing the necessary qualities for entrance and successful completion of the aspirant stage. Upon reviewing the recommendation, vote, and rationale of the committee, the diocesan bishop is the one who decides whether to admit the applicant into the aspirant stage. If an applicant is judged not to be ready but to be a suitable aspirant in the future, the director of formation should convey to the applicant various options for how he might prepare himself to achieve the basic entrance requirements. It is also essential for the director of formation to keep frequent contact with these potential candidates.

189.

With the acceptance of the applicant into aspirant formation, the admission process continues with an assessment of readiness for entrance into the candidate stage of formation. This phase of discernment extends throughout the entire aspirant formation process, thereby allowing ample opportunity for personal observations, dialogue, interviews, and additional assessments of each aspirant.

Norms

1. The inquirer who seeks consideration for ordination to the permanent diaconate needs to enter into dialogue with his parish, because it is the pastor who is required to present him initially for diaconal formation. (182)
2. A formal application process, as well as a committee on admission should be in place to review and nominate applicants. (183, 297)
3. As part of the application process, those charged with admission must—with appropriate care for confidentiality and manifestation of conscience—explore for the presence of canonical impediments to ordination. If canonical dispensations are required, these must be obtained before admission to aspirant formation. (184)
4. Required application documents are listed in paragraph 186. (186)
5. With acceptance into aspirant formation, the applicant's admission process continues with an assessment of readiness for entrance into the candidate stage of formation. (189)

[1] BNFPD, no. 29, citing PDV, no. 36.

[2] DMLPD, no. 49, citing St. Paul VI, Apostolic Letter Motu Proprio Sacrum Diaconatus Ordinem (June 18, 1967), no. 8, *www.vatican.va/content/paul-vi/en/motu_proprio/documents/hf_p-vi_motu-proprio_19670618_sacrum-diaconatus.html.*

[3] BNFPD, no. 32.

[4] BNFPD, nos. 31-33.

[5] "The 'art of accompaniment,' which teaches us to remove our sandals before the sacred ground of the other (cf. Ex 3:5). . . . must be steady and reassuring, reflecting our closeness and our compassionate gaze which also heals, liberates and encourages growth in the Christian life." EG, no. 169.

[6] BNFPD, no. 40; CIC, c. 233 §1.

[7] See this *National Directory*, chapter eight, no. 297, on committee on admission.

[8] See CIC, cc. 1040-1042. Canon 1041 enumerates irregularities as follows: "(1) a person who labors under some form of amentia or other psychic illness due to which, after experts have been consulted, he is judged unqualified to fulfill the ministry properly; (2) a person who has committed the delict of apostasy, heresy, or schism; (3) a person who has attempted marriage, even only civilly, while either impeded personally from entering marriage by a matrimonial bond, sacred orders, or a public perpetual vow of chastity, or with a woman bound by a valid marriage or restricted by the same type of vow; (3) a person who has committed voluntary homicide or procured a completed abortion and all those who positively cooperated in either; (4) a person who has mutilated himself or another gravely and maliciously or who has attempted suicide; (5) a person who has placed an act of orders reserved to those in the order of episcopate or presbyterate while either lacking that order or prohibited from its exercise by some declared or imposed canonical penalty"; and irregularities arising from public or occult delicts. Canon 1042 enumerates impediments as follows: "(2) a person who exercises an office or administration forbidden to clerics according to the norm of cann. 285 and 286 . . . ; (3) a neophyte unless he has been proven sufficiently in the judgment of the ordinary."

[9] BNFPD, no. 35. See no. 35 note 39.

[10] BNFPD, no. 70; see CIC, c. 1029.

[11] BNFPD, no. 70.

[12] If the information regarding Confirmation or marriage, if relevant, is not recorded on the baptismal record, separate certificates for Confirmation and marriage are to be obtained (CIC, cc. 1033, 1050 3°, 241 §2); relevant documents pertaining to a canonical declaration of nullity should also be obtained, if applicable. See this *National Directory*, no. 150.

[13] CIC, c. 1031 §3.

[14] The application form should provide information on his family; his religious, academic, employment, and service history; and a personal handwritten statement requesting admission into aspirant formation, indicating his motivation for seeking ordination to the diaconate, his willingness to pledge his service to the diocesan

Church, and his ability to fulfill the requirements of aspirant formation, if accepted. "It is necessary that this request be composed by the candidate personally and written out in his own hand and may not be a copied formulary, or worse, a photocopied text (see CIC, c. 1034 §1)." CL, enclosure II, no. 1.

[15] CL, enclosure I, no. 5.

[16] See note 14 in this chapter. This letter also should indicate her willingness to participate in the formation program as appropriate.

[17] CL, enclosure I, 11. Letters should be requested from priests, deacons, parishioners, and colleagues.

[18] CL, nos. 3, 4.

[19] CL, no. 10.

[20] CL, no. 4. See no. 8.

[21] See CIC, c. 265.

[22] The contact with the employer provides a way to inform him or her of the applicant's possible participation in a program of education that may require occasional time alterations in his work schedule.

[23] BNFPD, nos. 40, 45.

Chapter Five

Aspirant Stage of Diaconal Formation

I.
Introduction

190.

UPON COMPLETION of the initial inquiry process, the diocesan bishop may accept some inquirers into aspirancy. This aspirant stage of diaconal formation, as described in this *National Directory*, corresponds to the "propaedeutic period" required by the *Basic Norms for the Formation of Permanent Deacons* of the Congregation for Catholic Education.[1] The aspirant stage is primarily a time to discern the capability and readiness of an aspirant to be nominated to the diocesan bishop for acceptance as a candidate for diaconal ordination.[2]

191.

Those responsible for the aspirant stage of formation must be thoroughly familiar with the doctrinal understanding of the diaconate, including its ministry and life and the dimensions of formation, as described in the *Basic Norms for the Formation of Permanent Deacons* and this *Directory*. These components converge on a common goal: to enable the aspirant to demonstrate the possibility of a diaconal vocation and an appropriate level of readiness for eventual selection into candidate formation.[3]

192.

To create an environment conducive to adult Christian formation, the director of formation should maintain an aspirant handbook that details the components of the program, provides a rationale and guidance for assessment, and clearly delineates the expectations and responsibilities of the aspirant, including those regarding the wife of a married aspirant. This handbook is to be approved by the diocesan bishop.[4]

193.

Because of the aspirant's secular employment and personal and family commitments, appropriate attention is to be given to the implementation of a family life perspective in organizing the aspirant stage. In this regard, the most common formation models that have emerged in the United States of America organize formation meetings on various evenings, weekends, holidays, or a combination of such times. Different ways of organizing the aspirant formation stage are possible.[5] Since the director of formation, in collaboration with those who share in the responsibility for formation,[6] is expected to prepare for the diocesan bishop a declaration of readiness that profiles the aspirant's personality and provides a judgment of suitability for candidate formation and ultimately ordination, the aspirant stage of formation must be of an appropriate length.[7] In the diocesan Churches of the United States of America, the aspirant stage of formation ordinarily lasts two years.

194.

Although some aspects of the aspirant stage may be linked with other lay apostolate formation programs in a diocese, the aspirant stage must be a distinctive program that provides for a thorough discernment of a diaconal vocation. Therefore, it must include an appropriate initiation into diaconal spirituality; supervised pastoral experiences, especially among the poor and marginalized; and an adequate assessment of the aspirant's potential to be promoted to candidate formation and ultimately to ordination. The aspirant stage also must enable the formation personnel to create an environment in which the wife of a married aspirant can be appropriately prepared to give her consent to his continuation and, more essentially, to ascertain her compatibility with her husband's diaconal vocation and eventual ministry.[8]

195.

During this period of discernment, the aspirant is to be introduced to the study of theology, to a deeper knowledge of the spirituality and ministry of the deacon, and to a more attentive discernment of his call. This period is also a time to form an aspirant community with its own cycle of meetings and prayer. Finally, this period is to ensure the aspirant's regular participation in spiritual direction, to introduce him to the pastoral ministries of the diocesan Church, and to assist his family in their support of his formation.[9]

II.
The Dimensions of Formation in the Aspirant Stage

196.

At the aspirant level in formation, the following objectives are to be highlighted. These are presented in greater detail in chapter three, "Dimensions in the Formation of Deacons."

Human Dimension

197.

In his post-synodal apostolic exhortation *Pastores Dabo Vobis*, St. John Paul II quotes propositio 21 of the 1990 extraordinary synod of bishops: "The whole work of priestly formation would be deprived of its necessary foundation if it lacked a suitable human formation."[10] In a similar way, the same may be said about the human dimension of diaconal formation. The goal of a suitable human formation is to help the aspirant develop "his human personality in such a way that it becomes a bridge and not an obstacle for others in their meeting with Jesus Christ."[11] This might be more effectively achieved by giving attention to such areas as marriage development, emotional healing and maturing, integration of diaconal sacramental identity with life in a secular world after ordination, stress reduction, and virtue inculcation.

198.

The aspirant stage of formation is also a time for a married aspirant and his wife to assess the quality of their relationship and consider the ramifications that his possible ordination to the diaconate will have for their married life. For the single aspirant, it is a time to discern his capacity and receptivity for celibacy.

Spiritual Dimension

199.

The aspirant stage of formation must create an environment in which the individual is encouraged to grow in his personal relationship with Christ and in his commitment to the Church and its mission in the world. The goal of spiritual formation is "putting on the mind of Christ," thereby establishing and nurturing attitudes, habits, and practices that provide a foundation for the development of an authentic and ongoing spiritual life.

200.

Although it is clearly understood that the wife of the married aspirant is not seeking ordination, nevertheless, their marriage and family are involved in the discernment of his diaconal vocation. The aspirant and his wife need to realistically assess how her own life, church service, and family are affected and respected. The enrichment and deepening of the reciprocal and sacrificial love between husband and wife constitute perhaps the most meaningful way in which the wife of the aspirant is involved in the discernment of her husband's vocation.[12]

201.

The aspirant formation community plays a significant role in spiritual formation. The aspirant stage should include the following:

a. Regular participation in the Eucharist which goes beyond the fulfillment of obligations, Liturgy of the Hours, and the Sacrament of Penance[13]
b. Time scheduled for private prayer, meditation, and *lectio divina*
c. Devotions to the Virgin Mary and saints
d. Conferences and workshops on the meaning of authentic obedience, celibacy, and simplicity of life
e. Conferences on a Christian witness in both matrimonial and celibate life to the Church and world
f. An understanding and appreciation of the diaconal vocation, with an ability to articulate this call through the primary ministries of word, liturgy, and charity

g. An introduction and experience of the spiritual writings of our Catholic Tradition

202.

The aspirant's spiritual director is critical to the formation process. Therefore, this priest, who is to be approved by the diocesan bishop, must be well trained and knowledgeable about the diaconate. The spiritual director accompanies, supports, and challenges the aspirant in his ongoing conversion. The spiritual director assists the aspirant in his relationship with God and promotes his understanding that it is Christ who calls, the Church who affirms his diaconal vocation, and the diocesan bishop who responds to that affirmation by the imposition of hands.

203.

As collaborators in discerning the readiness of the aspirant to move into candidate formation, the parish and its pastor also should accompany the aspirant and his family by means of their prayers, support, and presence. In the aspirant stage of formation, the parish is the primary place to observe the aspirant's relational skills and his practice in pastoral service. The pastor, therefore, is to provide an assessment of the aspirant and his family. This assessment will further enable the formation staff to support and challenge the aspirant's discernment of his readiness to move into candidate formation.

Intellectual Dimension

204.

The objectives and content for intellectual formation at the aspirant level should communicate a deeper knowledge of the faith and the Word of God. During aspirancy a man should come to know Scripture as the living Word of God, learn to read it as prayer, listen to the movements of the Spirit within its content, and embrace it as the heart of a deacon's intellectual interest. Saturating aspirants in the living Word of God helps prepare them for the following years of more intensive study of its content as the source of doctrine and Catholic living. It would be appropriate to promote an in-depth and systematic study of the *Catechism of the Catholic Church* and to introduce the aspirant to the traditions of Catholic philosophy, spirituality, doctrine, and canon law, especially the doctrinal and canonical understanding of the diaconate and the threefold ministry of the deacon. The aspirant also should be taught how to participate in a theological reflection group and how to develop his ability to apply the Church's teaching on moral matters, including social teaching, to the pressing moral questions that emerge in pastoral ministry. Such intellectual pursuits assist those responsible for formation in assessing the aspirant's readiness for the academic rigors of candidate formation. Further, he should be made aware of the needs of the people of the diocesan Church, as well as of his own parish, and be made to understand *diakonia* as a descriptive word for the mission of the Church in the world. Workshops on family issues, personal health, time management, caregiving skills, and married and celibate spirituality all contribute to an aspirant's human, spiritual, and intellectual formation.

Pastoral Dimension

205.

The focus of the pastoral dimension in the aspirant stage of formation is ultimately the discernment of the aspirant's gifts for the threefold ministry of word, liturgy, and charity and of his capacity to make a lifelong commitment to these ministries. It also enables an assessment of his wife in her readiness to give consent and support to his vocation and ministry. Pastoral formation should introduce the aspirant to the practical services provided by the diocesan Church, and it should explore the core social issues confronting the diocese. Exemplary deacons or priests, approved by the diocesan bishop, should serve as mentors[14] inviting the aspirant to accompany, observe, assist, and reflect upon the specific diaconal ministries experienced.[15] Appropriate ecumenical pastoral experiences should be considered and implemented as opportunities emerge. Opportunities should also be provided, when possible, for involvement with the Jewish community and with representatives of other religions.

III.
Assessment for Nomination into the Candidate Stage of Formation

206.

The conclusion of the aspirant stage of formation is determined through a formal assessment conducted by the committee on admission. This occurs when the aspirant (with the consent of his wife, if married), with the express permission of those responsible for his formation, makes a written petition to the diocesan bishop for admission to candidacy.

207.

When the decision to petition for candidacy is determined, the following documents are to be prepared:

a. A personal, handwritten, and signed letter prepared for the diocesan bishop by the aspirant requesting admission to the candidate stage of formation, as well as the reception of the Rite of Admission to Candidacy.[16] In his letter, the aspirant must state his motivation and reasons for the requests. If he is married, he must indicate his awareness of the impact of diaconal ordination and ministry on his marriage and family; he also must state that he has received the consent of his wife. If he is not married, he should indicate his awareness of the meaning of diaconal ordination and ministry, as well as his understanding of and ability to live the requirement of perpetual celibacy, which also applies to a married deacon should his wife predecease him following ordination or in the event of a subsequent civil divorce.[17]
b. A personal, handwritten, and signed letter of consent prepared by the married aspirant's wife.[18]

208.

The following assessments are to be conducted and maintained in the aspirant's and candidate's permanent file:

a. Written pastoral supervisors' assessments and reports
b. Written parochial assessments prepared by the pastor and parish staff
c. If applicable, a written assessment by the rector of any previous house of formation, or a similar report from the director of any

diaconal formation program in which the aspirant or candidate previously participated

d. In a case where an aspirant comes from another diocesan Church, a letter of recommendation from his previous pastor, as well as consultation with that Church's vocations and diaconate offices
e. An assessment of the aspirant's or candidate's aptitude for preaching, catechizing, and evangelization
f. A personal assessment from the director of formation, prepared for the committee on admission, following the model prescribed by the Congregation for Divine Worship and the Discipline of the Sacraments[19]

209.

Each aspirant will be interviewed by the committee on admission to appraise his readiness for admission into the candidate stage of formation. The committee will also meet separately with the wife of a married aspirant to ascertain her level of consent and support for her husband's promotion into candidate formation. Finally, the committee will review all pertinent data on the aspirant. The vote of each member and the rationale for the vote is to be recorded. The director of formation, on behalf of the committee, will prepare "a declaration which outlines the profile of the [aspirant's personality] . . . and a judgment of suitability."[20] This declaration, accompanied by the individual vote and rationale of each member of the committee, is prepared for the diocesan bishop, who selects those to be admitted to candidate formation. A copy of the declaration and the diocesan bishop's letter to the aspirant regarding his acceptance into candidacy, as well as a copy of the personal, handwritten, and signed letter of consent prepared by the married aspirant's wife, is placed in the petitioner's personal file.[21]

IV.
The Rite of Admission to Candidacy

210.

The Rite of Admission to Candidacy is to be celebrated as soon as possible after the aspirant is admitted. In this rite, the one who aspires to ordination publicly manifests his will to offer himself to God and the Church to exercise a sacred order. In this way, he is admitted into the ranks of candidates for the diaconate.[22] "Enrollment among the candidates for the diaconate does not constitute any right necessarily to receive diaconal ordination. It is a first official recognition of the positive signs of the vocation to the diaconate, which must be confirmed in the subsequent years of formation."[23]

211.

Because of its public character and its ecclesial significance, this rite should be celebrated in a proper manner, preferably on a Sunday or feast day. Special consideration should be given to the inclusion of the candidate's wife and children, as well as to the cultural traditions represented.

212.

Aspirants accepted for candidacy—and, if married, their wives—should prepare themselves for the reception of the rite through a spiritual retreat.[24] It will usually be helpful for wives to participate in the retreat, although during portions of the retreat it will usually be helpful to provide the opportunity for separate treatment of the respective roles of each in the vocation of the husband to the diaconate. After the celebration of the Rite of Admission to Candidacy, a certificate indicating the reception, date, and place, as well as the name of the presiding prelate, must be prepared and signed by the chancellor and officially sealed. This document is to be maintained carefully in the candidate's personal file and recorded in the diocesan book on ministries and ordinations.[25]

Norms

1. The aspirant stage is primarily a time to discern the readiness of the aspirant to be nominated to the diocesan bishop for acceptance into the candidate stage of diaconal formation. (190)
2. A handbook should be available to aspirants detailing the components of the program, rationale and guidance for assessment, and

the expectations and responsibilities of the aspirants, including the wife of any married aspirant. (192)

3. The aspirant phase, which will ordinarily last two years, involves discernment with emphasis on human elements, spiritual readiness, intellectual capacity, and pastoral abilities. (193)
4. The aspirant stage must create an environment in which the wife of a married aspirant can give her consent to her husband's continuance in formation. More essentially, it must ascertain her compatibility with her husband's diaconal vocation and eventual ministry. (194)
5. The objectives and content for intellectual formation at the aspirant level should communicate a deeper knowledge of the faith and Church Tradition, as well as diaconal theology and spirituality, and should include meetings for prayer, instructions, and moments of reflection that will ensure the objective nature of vocational discernment. (204)
6. The conclusion of the aspirant stage of formation is determined through a formal assessment conducted by the committee on admission. (206)
7. A copy of the personal, handwritten, and signed letter prepared for the diocesan bishop by the aspirant requesting admission to the candidate stage of formation, as well as a copy of the personal, handwritten, and signed letter of consent prepared by the married aspirant's wife, is to be maintained carefully in the candidate's personal file. (207, 209)
8. After the aspirant stage is completed, the aspirant is selected by the diocesan bishop. The aspirant then begins the candidate stage of formation with the Rite of Admission to Candidacy, which is to be celebrated as soon as possible and in a proper manner. (210)
9. A retreat should precede the Rite of Admission to Candidacy. (212)
10. A certificate indicating the reception, date, and place, as well as the name of the presiding prelate, must be prepared and signed by the chancellor and officially sealed. This document is to be maintained carefully in the candidate's personal file and recorded in the diocesan book on ministries and ordinations. (212)

[1] BNFPD, nos. 41-44. "With admission among the aspirants to diaconate there begins a propaedeutic period . . . [in which] the aspirants will be introduced to a deeper knowledge of theology, of spirituality and of the ministry of deacon and they will be led to a more attentive discernment of their call." The propaedeutic period may be compared to the pre-seminary program in priestly formation or postulancy in religious life.

[2] BNFPD, nos. 41-44.

[3] See CL, nos. 1-2.

[4] BNFPD, no. 16.

[5] BNFPD, no. 51.

[6] BNFPD, no. 44 (formation team, supervisors, and pastor).

[7] BNFPD, nos. 41, 44.

[8] BNFPD, no. 37.

[9] BNFPD, nos. 41-44.

[10] PDV, no. 43.

[11] PDV, no. 43.

[12] ADUS.

[13] These recommendations presuppose that he is already meeting his obligations to attend weekly Sunday Mass and all Holy Days of Obligation. See CIC, c. 1247.

[14] When this *National Directory* uses the term "mentor," it is referring to the "tutor" from the *Basic Norms for the Formation of Permanent Deacons*. See BNFPD, nos. 20, 22, 42, 70.

[15] BNFPD, no. 22.

[16] See CIC, c. 1034 §1.

[17] See this *National Directory*, nos. 75-78, 225.

[18] CL, enclosure I, no. 14. The wife must declare her consent for his petition to enter into candidacy formation; she also should clearly state her understanding of the meaning of diaconal ordination and ministry and its impact on their marriage and family.

[19] CL. Shared resources are available from the Secretariat for Clergy, Consecrated Life, and Vocations at the USCCB and from the National Association of Diaconate Directors.

[20] BNFPD, no. 44.

[21] CL, enclosure III, especially nos. 4, 6, and 8.

[22] St. Paul VI, Apostolic Letter *Ministeria Quaedam* (August 15, 1972), *www.vatican.va/content/paul-vi/la/motu_proprio/documents/hf_p-vi_motu-proprio_19720815_ministeria-quaedam.html* (Latin only). Membership in the clerical state occurs at ordination and not at the time of candidacy.

[23] BNFPD, no. 48.

[24] BNFPD, no. 47.

[25] CL, enclosure I.

Chapter Six

Candidate Stage of Diaconal Formation

I.
Introduction

213.

THE CANDIDATE STAGE of initial formation is the occasion to confirm a man's diaconal vocation[1] and prepare for ordination. Throughout this stage of formation, the candidate himself assumes the primary responsibility for his discernment and development.[2] "Self-formation does not imply isolation . . . or independence from formators, but responsibility and dynamism in responding with generosity to God's call, valuing to the highest the people and tools which Providence puts at one's disposition. Self-formation has its roots in a firm determination to grow in life according to the Spirit and in conformity with the vocation received."[3]

II.
The Length of the Candidate Stage of Formation

214.

In accord with the *Code of Canon Law*, the *Basic Norms for the Formation of Permanent Deacons* by the Congregation for Catholic Education specifies that the candidate stage of diaconal formation "must last at least three years, in addition to the *propaedeutic period*, for all candidates."[4] Readiness for ordination is assessed annually by both the candidate and formation personnel to ascertain what level of achievement the candidate has reached in his understanding of the diaconal vocation, its rights and its obligations, his growth in the spiritual life, his competency in required diaconal knowledge and skills, his practical experience in pastoral ministry, and his witness of human and affective maturity. If he is married, a discernment of his wife's readiness is also to be made. In a Circular Letter directed to diocesan ordinaries on assessing the readiness of candidates for ordination, the Congregation for Divine Worship and the Discipline of the Sacraments recalls that "St. Paul's admonition remains true for the Church today, as it did in his own time: 'Do not be hasty in the laying-on of hands.'"[5]

215.

Regarding the precise number of hours for lectures, seminars, and related educational activities specified in the *Basic Norms for the Formation of Permanent Deacons*,[6] the objective is to guarantee the planning and implementation of an integral and substantive program of initial formation that adequately prepares a candidate to represent the Church as a deacon. A substantive program includes not only class preparation, participation, and attendance, but also seminars, workshops, pastoral placements, theological reflection, shared opportunities for spiritual growth (e.g., liturgical celebrations and prayer, spiritual conferences, retreats), individual spiritual direction, and other formation experiences. Whenever possible, the candidate should receive spiritual direction in the language with which he is most comfortable. Diocesan compliance with this requirement and others as specified in the *Basic Norms for the Formation of Permanent Deacons* and in this *National Directory* may be verified by the review of its formation program by CCLV.

III.
Formation Environments

216.

The communities in which the candidate participates influence the formation process.[7] Those entrusted with initial formation must take care to assess the value of these environments as resources for discerning, supporting, and nurturing a diaconal vocation.

Candidate Formation Community

217.

The candidate community should become primarily an integrating experience where dialogue and collaborative activity provide a unique opportunity for adults to discern the activity of the Holy Spirit in their lives and experiences.

218.

To create an environment conducive to adult Christian formation, the director of formation should maintain and make readily accessible a candidate handbook that details the components of the program; provides the rationale, criteria, and guidance for assessments, especially regarding readiness for institution into the ministries of lector and acolyte and, ultimately, for ordination to the diaconate; and clearly delineates the expectations and responsibilities of the candidate, including the wife of a married candidate. This handbook is to be approved by the diocesan bishop.[8]

The Community of Deacons

219.

The community of deacons can be a "precious support in the discernment of vocation, in human growth, in the initiation to the spiritual life, in theological study and pastoral experience."[9] Scheduled opportunities for conversation and shared pastoral experiences between a candidate and a deacon, as well as meetings between the wife of a candidate and the wife of a deacon, can mutually sustain their enthusiasm and realism about the diaconate. Some exemplary deacons in addition to priests should be appointed by the diocesan bishop to serve as mentors to individual candidates or a small group of candidates.[10]

The Parish Community

220.

The parish community is an essential extension of the formation community. Through its prayer and support, the parish "makes the faithful aware of this ministry, [and] gives to the candidate a strong aid to his vocational discernment."[11]

The Family Community

221.

The family is the primary community accompanying the candidate on the formative journey. For married candidates, the communion of life and love, established by the marriage covenant and consecrated by the Sacrament of Matrimony, offers a singular contribution to the formation process.[12] The single candidate's family also contributes to his formation; those responsible for implementing the formation process should consult with the single candidate to ascertain the strength of his support from his family and friends in order to ensure that his vocation is also encouraged and fostered.

The Marketplace Community

222.

Those responsible for implementing the formation process are to thoroughly determine the candidate's employment situation—his *marketplace* formation community—and its impact on his preparation, discernment, and readiness for ordination to the diaconate. St. John Paul II stressed the importance of this particular formation environment at a plenary assembly of the Congregation for the Clergy: "It is the circumstances of his life—prudently evaluated by the candidate himself and by the diocesan bishop, before ordination—which should, if necessary, be adapted to the exercise of his ministry by facilitating it in every way."[13]

IV.
The Dimensions of Formation in the Candidate Stage

223.

Those responsible for the candidate stage of formation should be thoroughly familiar with the doctrinal understanding of the diaconate, the ministry and life of deacons, the dimensions of formation, and the discernment of a diaconal vocation described earlier in this *National Directory*. These components have a common goal: to enable the candidate to demonstrate an appropriate level of preparedness for nomination to the diocesan bishop for ordination to the diaconate. It is essential that those responsible for the formation of candidates receive training to fulfill their responsibilities. The following descriptions highlight specific components to be emphasized.

Human Dimension

224.

The aim of the human dimension of the candidate stage of formation is to continue to build on the human qualities already discerned during the aspirancy period (see paragraphs 197 and 198 above), developing them and adding skills necessary for an effective and responsible diaconal ministry. Emphasis is to be placed upon his relational and collaborative qualities and skills, especially his strengths and limitations in this regard. During the candidate stage, the candidate also acknowledges his giftedness and develops the habit of authentic self-criticism in light of the Gospel. He must learn how to integrate his personal, familial, work, and ministerial responsibilities.

Spiritual Dimension

225.

One of the primary objectives of the spiritual dimension of the candidate stage of formation is "to assist the candidate in achieving a spiritual integration" of his life, family, work, and apostolic service. The spiritual goal is to help the candidate to increase in holiness by "equipping and motivating" him to lay a foundation upon which he may "continue [his] spiritual growth after ordination." Throughout his formation, the candidate is "to secure the assistance of a . . . [spiritual director], to cultivate regular patterns of prayer and sacramental participation, and . . . to reflect spiritually on [his] ministry."[15] As a complement to individual spiritual direction, it would also be useful for small groups of candidates to engage together in theological reflection "on the challenges and opportunities of their ministries" in relationship to the Gospel and magisterial teaching.[16] Further, throughout the formation process, it is expedient that the candidate's spiritual director and those responsible for his formation ascertain the candidate's understanding, willingness, and capacity to accept the Church's discipline regarding perpetual celibacy not merely among those who are not married, but also among married men who will be required to embrace this ecclesiastical discipline in widowhood or divorce (even with a subsequent declaration of nullity). Dispensations from the requirement of celibacy cannot be presumed.

226.

The goals of the spiritual dimension during the candidate stage of formation include the following:

a. To help each candidate to increase in holiness by deepening and cultivating his commitment to Christ and the Church
b. To strengthen his love for the study of the Word of God and his desire to pray with Scripture throughout a lifetime of ministry
c. To assist the candidate in confirming his vocation to the diaconate
d. To help him deepen his prayer life—personal, familial, communal, and liturgical—and to instill in the candidate a commitment to pray daily for the Church, especially through the Liturgy of the Hours
e. To strengthen the personal charisms he has already demonstrated in his life
f. To help him integrate his new commitment to prepare for the diaconate with his previous commitments to his family and professional employment
g. To acquaint him with the relationship between spirituality and his commitment to the Church's ministry of charity, which includes the promotion of justice
h. To acquaint him with Catholic classical and contemporary spiritual writings and the witness of the saints
i. To prepare him for the challenges of spiritual leadership that his ministry will entail

Intellectual Dimension

227.

The intellectual dimension of the candidate stage of formation must be carefully designed. A description of the core content for the candidate can be found in norms 5 through 12 at the end of this chapter. The intellectual dimension is "oriented toward ministry, providing the candidate with the knowledge and appreciation of the faith that he needs in order to carry out his ministry"[17] of word, liturgy, and charity. The course of study is to be complete and must be in harmony with the magisterial teaching of the Church so that the future deacon is a "reliable witness of the faith and spokes[man] for the Church's teaching."[18] It should also take into account the specific diaconal services the candidate will provide in the communities that he will be appointed to serve, as well as topics that reflect the specific concerns of the Church in the United States of America. The intellectual dimension must equip the candidate for his leadership and participation in the new evangelization and for his effective heralding of the Gospel in today's society. Studies of Sacred Scripture, Liturgy, canon law, marriage and family, lay spirituality, social doctrine, evangelization, and missiology are to be given prominence.

Pastoral Dimension

228.

"During formation, engagement in a wide diversity of" pastoral placements, "at least on a limited basis, will not only give the candidate a greater awareness of the needs and mission of the [diocesan] Church, but will assist in the discernment and development of his own . . . talents and gifts."[19] These pastoral experiences "should provide an opportunity for theological reflection, as well as occasions to translate" intellectual knowledge into pastoral service.[20] A description of the core content for the formation of candidates can be found in norms 13 through 15 at the end of this chapter. "Competent, objective," and supportive supervisors will be required in order to help the candidate to achieve these goals.[21] The diocesan Church "must be committed to the [selection and] preparation of skillful . . . supervisors who possess pastoral experience, [training] . . . in the art of supervision, and . . . [the ability to assist] mature men with [diverse] life experiences."[22] During candidacy, emphasis also is to be given to the study of the role of culture in human, spiritual, and pastoral formation. Further, the pastoral dimension is to provide a significant grounding in the social justice teaching of the Church.

V.
The Assessment of Candidates

Formational Assessment

229.

A primary opportunity for assessment of the candidate occurs within an actual pastoral setting. Can the candidate do that which his training is preparing him to do? Does the way in which he presents himself in pastoral ministry show, for example, an integrated and balanced sense of the ecclesiology of the Second Vatican Council and an understanding of his role within the Church and in its mission of service? Does the way he participates in and leads prayerful gatherings of his community give evidence of liturgical knowledge and cultural sensitivity? Can he demonstrate a properly formed conscience and moral sensitivity? Can he form others in a convincing, sound manner? Each diocese should find those assessment methods that best measure the progress of each candidate in appropriating the diaconal identity and mission. In the interest of transparency and fairness, the assessment methods/benchmarks chosen by the diocesan bishop and formation faculty are to be well articulated and provided in writing with clear explanations to the candidates, so they are aware of them before evaluations.

230.

A further means of assessing the candidate is theological reflection on his pastoral assignment. Here the role of the peer community is of utmost importance. The candidate reports on his pastoral assignment, and the community enables him to reflect upon the human, spiritual, intellectual, and pastoral dimensions of his actions. This format greatly fosters the sense of partnership in assessment.

231.

Another opportunity for assessment lies in the classroom, where pastoral practice can be simulated, whether through case study, role playing, or some form of pastoral problem solving. Although not empowered by the sense of immediacy or by connection to a real incident, such simulations can be designed to explore any number of competencies in a structured and progressive program.

232.

To enable assessment of the candidate's intellectual formation, traditional examinations or academic papers are necessary, as prescribed by the *Basic Norms for the Formation of Permanent Deacons* of the Congregation for Catholic Education. Plagiarism is to be explained and diligently confronted.

233.

A sense of partnership can be fostered by allowing the candidate to present a portfolio of his accomplishments, to design a variety of ways in which he may demonstrate his readiness, or to engage in a collaborative study venture with those charged with his formation.

234.

A comprehensive and integrative seminar, such as those used in professional education, is recommended as a model to determine the level of assimilation and achievement of the candidate at the completion of his theological course of study. This model fulfills the requirement of a comprehensive review as required by the *Basic Norms for the Formation of Permanent Deacons*.[23] The faculty facilitators of the seminar evaluate how effectively the individual candidate is "able to explain his faith and bring to maturity a lively ecclesial conscience,"[24] how he has acquired "the capacity to read a situation and an adequate inculturation of the Gospel,"[25] and how successfully he has used "communication techniques and group dynamics, the ability to speak in public, and [the ability] to give guidance and counsel."[26] In such seminars, typically centered on case studies of a pastoral nature, the candidate has an opportunity to explore pastoral solutions in the presence of his peers, formation faculty, and pastoral supervisors. In the seminar, he is called upon to demonstrate not only an intellectual understanding of theology, but also its application in pastoral practice. He gives and receives feedback, thus demonstrating his competency in such areas as communication and his ability to work constructively within a group. In addition, his pastoral worldview is exposed and assessed, and his "pastoral intuition" is honored and challenged. The goal of this comprehensive and integrative seminar is always to project how the candidate will live a diaconal lifestyle and ministry. In this way it serves as a comprehensive assessment of the deacon's practical intellectual readiness for ministry.

Vocational Assessment

235.

Interviews should be scheduled regularly with candidates and their families, their pastors and pastoral supervisors, members of the faculty, and mentors. The director of formation and those who collaborate with him should gather at regularly scheduled times to stay informed about a candidate's progress. They should address concerns and become collectively aware of their common collaborative role in assisting, counseling, and assessing the candidate. This responsibility should be regarded as their most important task. Due care must be taken, however, to preserve the confidentiality of spiritual direction in these proceedings.

236.

The responsibility of the team of formators culminates in the preparation of a yearly written report on each candidate. This report, which is to be presented to the diocesan bishop, provides a synthesis of the candidate's achievements and limitations, particularly in reference to his human, spiritual, intellectual, and pastoral readiness for continuation in the formation process and, ultimately, for nomination to ordination.[27] This written assessment should include an estimation of an unmarried candidate's capacity to lead a perpetual chaste and celibate life. For a married candidate, it should present an appraisal of his family's stability and capacity to support his vocation, especially addressing the status of his wife's readiness. Each year, the number of affirmative and negative votes of the formation team regarding the continuance or separation of the candidate from formation is to be recorded. If there are abstentions, they are to be explained.[28] The diocesan bishop expects the objective and critical judgment of those who collaborate with him in formation. This report should reflect a clear consensus among those who have been involved with the candidate's training and formation. The written report is to be maintained in the candidate's personal file, where accumulated reports can be compared to ascertain patterns of growth or regression, as well as new areas for affirmation or concern.

237.

The director of formation must transmit this report verbally to the candidate. It should be made available to the candidate's spiritual director, whose "task is that of discerning the workings of the Spirit in the soul of those called and, at that same time, of accompanying and supporting their ongoing conversion."[29] It may be helpful to share the report with the candidate's proper pastor, if he did not participate in the formal review. Finally, the director of formation also will share this report with the committee on admission, especially in its deliberations regarding admittance to the ministries of lector and acolyte and regarding ordination to the diaconate.

238.

If a candidate does not possess the necessary human, spiritual, intellectual, or pastoral qualities that will allow him to minister as a deacon in a collaborative and effective way, it is only just to the individual and to the Church to communicate this to him as early as possible and in a constructive manner. Sometimes the evaluation consensus clearly indicates termination of formation or a refusal of recommendation for advancement to ministries or ordination. Candidates who lack positive qualities for continuing in the formation process should not nourish false hopes and illusions that could damage themselves and their families, their peers, or the Church. Therefore, with the approval of the diocesan bishop, the candidate should be advised to leave formation. Although no one has a right to continue in formation or a right to be ordained, in justice and with pastoral sensitivity the reasons for this decision should be shared with the candidate, and a fair hearing should be given to his own assessment of the situation, as well as to that of others who may wish to speak on his behalf.

239.

In situations of doubt about the readiness of a candidate to be called to ordination, or about his progress in achieving appropriate levels of adult formation, the diocesan bishop may consider a period of probation. This time, however, should be specifically limited, not left open-ended. Likewise, appropriate supervision is absolutely necessary during this period to bring about needed growth and provide suitable information on which to base a judgment. It will be helpful, therefore, to prepare a written plan of action indicating the goals to be achieved, the actions that will be followed to meet the goals, and the means of evaluating and verifying the achievement of the goals. This written plan should further specify the supervisor who will accompany the candidate through the process. It must be understood that in such situations, the burden of proof of readiness for ordination rests with the candidate, and doubt is resolved in favor of the Church.

240.

Paralleling the process indicated for the external forum, spiritual direction is similarly crucial to the candidate's discernment. The individual's spiritual director should receive the information regarding this period of probation; and through internal forum, he should assist the individual through regularly scheduled meetings.

VI.
Scrutinies for Institution into the Ministries of Lector and Acolyte and Ordination to the Diaconate

241.

In accord with the Circular Letter from the Congregation for Divine

Worship and the Discipline of the Sacraments (November 28, 1997), scrutinies are to take place prior to institution into the ministries of lector and acolyte[30] and prior to ordination to the diaconate.[31]

242.

Required documentation and procedures for institution into the ministries of lector and acolyte include the following (these are to be followed when petitioning for institution into the ministry of lector and repeated when petitioning for the ministry of acolyte):

a. The candidate handwrites his request to be admitted to the specific ministry. This request must be composed by the candidate personally and written in his own hand; it "may not be copied formulary, or worse, a photocopied text."[32]
b. The director of formation prepares a personal report, which should be detailed, making use of the model found in the Circular Letter and which should include the candidate's annual self and peer assessments.
c. The candidate's proper pastor is consulted, and he writes a letter of recommendation.
d. The committee on admission interviews the candidate's wife, if he is married, to ascertain her understanding of her husband's institution into these ministries as part of the formation discernment process.
e. Faculty and pastoral assignment supervisors provide assessments of the candidate.
f. A smaller team from the committee on admission interviews the candidate to ascertain his knowledge of the ministry to be received and his capacity to fulfill its responsibilities.
g. Other documentation is provided, as requested by the committee.[33]

243.

"It should not be permitted that the candidate's family or the parish community presume his future Ordination" before the call of the competent authority, especially by mailing invitations or making other preparations for the ordination celebration. "Behavior of this kind can constitute a form of psychological pressure that must be avoided in every way possible."[34] The diocesan bishop will select those to be ordained to the diaconate and will set the date and other specifications for the ordination. It is assumed that the diocesan bishop will do this in consultation with the ordinand and his family.

244.

Required documentation and procedures for ordination to the diaconate include the following (these are to be followed when petitioning for ordination to the diaconate):

a. Before petitioning for ordination, the candidate keeps in mind that there must be an interval of at least six months between the conferring of the ministry of acolyte and ordination to the diaconate.[35]
b. The candidate submits a written request to be admitted to the Order of Deacons. This request must be composed by the candidate personally and written in his own hand; it "may not be copied formulary, or worse, a photocopied text."[36] The candidate's handwritten request must attest "that he will receive the sacred order of his own accord and freely will devote himself perpetually to the ecclesiastical ministry."[37]
c. The candidate's wife writes and signs a statement in which she declares her consent to the ordination petition of her husband and makes clear her own understanding of the meaning of diaconal ministry.[38]
d. The director of formation prepares a personal report, which should be detailed, making use of the model proposed in the Circular Letter, and which should include the annual vocational assessment report.[39]
e. The director, in compliance with the *Code of Canon Law*, canons 1032 and 1050 1°, must present a certificate verifying the candidate's completion of all required studies.
f. The candidate's proper pastor is consulted, and he writes a letter of recommendation.
g. The committee on admission interviews the candidate to ascertain his knowledge of the Order of Deacons to be received and its obligations and rights; his understanding and willingness, if single or widowed, to accept the Church's discipline regarding perpetual

celibate chastity; his understanding and willingness, if married, to embrace the magisterial teaching on marriage and sexuality, as well as its ecclesiastical discipline in widowhood; and his understanding of the rights and obligations of a cleric and his capacity to fulfill these responsibilities.

h. The committee interviews the wife of a married candidate to ascertain her willingness to support his petition and to live as the wife of a deacon.
i. The canonical banns are published within a sufficiently extended period of time in advance of ordination in the parishes where the candidate has had an extended residence or presence in his formation ministries.[40]
j. The candidate provides a recent photograph and biographical information for use in the publicizing of his ordination.
k. Other documentation is provided, as requested by the committee.[41]

245.

A collegial session of the committee on admission is to be scheduled for these assessments.[42] Having consulted the committee, the diocesan bishop will select those to be admitted to each specific ministry and those to be called to ordination.

Rite of Institution into the Ministry of Lector and Ministry of Acolyte

246.

It is appropriate for a retreat or a day for reflection to precede the reception of the specific ministry. Whenever possible, this should be provided in the language with which the candidate is most comfortable. It will usually be helpful to wives to participate in the retreat, although during portions of the retreat it will usually be helpful to provide the opportunity for separate treatment of the respective roles of each in the vocation of the husband to the diaconate. The conferral of the ministry should be celebrated on a Sunday or feast day, according to the rite of *the Roman Pontifical.* These rites are public celebrations with ecclesial significance.[43] Special attention should be given to the participation of the wives and children of married candidates. The ministry of lector is to be conferred first. "It is appropriate that a certain period of time elapse between the conferring of the lectorate [rite of lector] and acolytate [rite of acolyte] in such a way that the candidate may exercise the ministry he has received."[44]

247.

After the reception of the ministry, a certificate indicating the ministry received, date, place, and conferring prelate should be prepared and signed by the chancellor of the diocese and officially sealed. This document is to be kept in the candidate's personal file and noted in the diocesan book of ministries and ordinations.

Rite of Ordination to the Diaconate

248.

An interval of at least six months must elapse between the conferring of the ministry of acolyte and ordination to the diaconate.[45] Further, a canonical retreat of at least five days must precede the ordination.[46] It will usually be helpful to wives to participate in the retreat, although during portions of the retreat it will usually be helpful to provide the opportunity for separate treatment of the respective roles of each in the vocation of the husband to the diaconate. Prior to ordination to the diaconate, the ordinand must make the Profession of Faith and the Oath of Fidelity in the presence of the diocesan bishop or his delegate and must sign them by his own hand.[47] He must take the Oath of Fidelity and make a personal declaration concerning his freedom to receive sacred ordination, as well as his own clear awareness of the obligations and commitments implied by that ordination. For married candidates, this includes an understanding that if his wife were to die, he would live a life of celibacy. An unmarried candidate must make a declaration regarding the obligation of sacred celibacy; this declaration must be written in the candidate's own handwriting and expressed in his own words. A married candidate, should his wife predecease him after ordination, is bound to the celibate state for the remainder of his life.[48] Prior to ordination the diocesan bishop will issue a formal letter of call to ordination. All of these documents are to be carefully preserved in the candidate's personal file.[49]

249.

It is preferable to celebrate the ordination in the cathedral church on a Sunday or feast day, according to the rite of *the Roman Pontifical*, inviting the diocesan Church's full participation. "During the rite special attention should be given to the participation of the wives and children of the married ordinands."[50]

250.

After the ordination, a certificate should be prepared containing the date, place, and name of the ordaining prelate. It should be signed and sealed by the chancellor. This information also should be recorded in the diocesan book of ministries and ordinations. The certificate, together with the letter of petition and the diocesan bishop's letter of call to ordination, should be enclosed in the newly ordained deacon's personal and permanent file. The newly ordained deacon should also receive a written testimonial to his ordination.[51] The newly ordained deacon's personal and permanent file should be transferred, as soon after the ordination as is convenient, from the formation office to a permanent location among the curia records in the diocesan chancery. The director of formation or someone designated by the diocesan bishop must also notify the church in which the newly ordained was baptized so that the information regarding the ordination may be included in that church's baptismal-sacramental records.[52] The parish of Baptism may notify the director of formation when the information has been recorded.

Norms

1. The candidate stage of formation must last at least three years, which does not include the two-year aspirant stage. (214)
2. Regarding the intellectual dimension and the number of hours of lectures, seminars, and related educational activities specified in the *Basic Norms for the Formation of Permanent Deacons*, the objective of this requirement is to guarantee the planning and implementation of an integral and substantive program of formation that adequately prepares a candidate to represent the Church as an ordained minister. (215)
3. The human dimension of this stage of formation continues to

develop the human qualities already discerned during the aspirant stage, adding necessary skills for an effective and responsible diaconal ministry. (224)

4. The spiritual dimension of this stage happens through the candidate's meeting regularly with his spiritual director and those responsible for formation. The goals are for the candidate to increase in holiness; to deepen his prayer life through the Eucharist, the Sacrament of Penance, the Liturgy of the Hours, and devotions; and to acquaint himself with the Catholic spiritual tradition reflected in classic and modern spiritual writings. (225, 226)
5. The intellectual dimension of this stage of formation introduces the candidate to the essentials of Christian doctrine and practice, including the core areas of theology faithful to the Magisterium of the Church and based on Scripture and Tradition, the documents of the Second Vatican Council, the *Catechism of the Catholic Church*, and the *General Directory for Catechesis*. (132, 227)
6. From Scripture, the core studies should include the major themes and content of the Old and New Testaments: Christian Scriptures, their stages of formation, and their place at the heart of Scripture. Attention should be given to the biblical themes of justice and peace that root and foster Catholic social teaching. (133, 227)
7. From dogmatic theology, the core studies should include fundamental theology, the Trinity, Christology, Creation and the nature of sin, redemption, grace and the human person, ecclesiology (both the Latin and Eastern Catholic Churches *sui iuris*), ecumenism and interreligious dialogue, sacraments (especially the Sacrament of Holy Orders and the theology and the relationship of the diaconate to the episcopate, the presbyterate, and the laity), eschatology, Mariology, missiology, and Catholic evangelization. (133, 227)
8. From moral theology, the core studies should include fundamental moral theology, medical-moral ethics, marriage and family, sexuality, and social-ministerial ethics. The social teaching of the Church should be presented substantially. (133, 227)
9. From historical studies, the candidate should be introduced to the history of the Church through the ages with an emphasis on patristics. The candidates should be familiar with the multicultural

origins of the Church in the United States of America. (133, 227)

10. From canon law, the core studies should include a general introduction and those canons specific to the exercise of the diaconate, in particular marriage legislation, as well as the obligations and rights of clerics and the canons relevant to diocesan structures and the administration of temporal goods. In addition, a provision should be made for instruction on the USCCB's *Charter for the Protection of Children and Young People* and *Essential Norms for Diocesan/Eparchial Policies for Dealing with Allegations of Sexual Abuse of Minors by Priests or Deacons*. (133, 227)
11. From spirituality, the core studies should include an introduction to spirituality, to spiritual direction, to lay spirituality, and to a selection of classic spiritual writers. (132, 227)
12. From Liturgy, the core studies should include an introduction to Liturgy and to the historical, spiritual, and juridical aspects of Liturgy. (133, 227)
13. Practica for the ministry of liturgy should include specific training in the functions of the deacon during the Eucharist, Baptism, Rite of Christian Initiation of Adults, the Sacrament of Matrimony, the rites of Christian burial, and other liturgical ministries of the diaconate. (138, 139)
14. From homiletics, deacons should have courses specifically aimed at preparing and delivering homilies. (139)
15. Pastoral formation must include a wide diversity of pastoral services, including opportunities for theological reflection. Attention should be given to the study of the role of culture in human and spiritual formation. (135, 138, 140, 142, 228)
16. A comprehensive seminar should be conducted at the end of the candidate stage of formation to enhance the candidates' integration of learning and to assess their readiness for ordination. (234)
17. The responsibility of formation personnel culminates in the preparation of a yearly written report on each aspirant and candidate that will be presented to the diocesan bishop through the director of formation. (236)
18. The director of formation must verbally transmit a yearly report to each candidate. (237)

19. Scrutinies are to take place prior to institution into the ministries of lector and acolyte and prior to ordination to the diaconate. (241)
20. A retreat or day of reflection should precede the reception of the ministries of lector and acolyte. (246)
21. An interval of at least six months must elapse between the conferring of the ministry of acolyte and ordination to the diaconate. (248)
22. A canonical retreat of at least five days must precede ordination. (248)
23. After the institution into each ministry and after ordination, a certificate should be prepared containing the date, place, and name of the installing or ordaining prelate. It should be signed and sealed by the chancellor. This information also should be recorded in the diocesan book of ministries and ordinations. The director of formation should also notify the church in which the newly ordained deacon was baptized so that the information regarding the ordination may be included in that church's baptismal-sacramental records. The parish of Baptism may notify the director of formation when the information has been recorded. The newly ordained deacon's personal and permanent file should also include a copy of the diocesan bishop's letter of call to ordination as well as the written testimonial of ordination. All of these canonical documents should be transferred, as soon after the ordination as is convenient, from the formation office to a permanent location among the curia records in the diocesan chancery. (250)

---

[1] BNFPD, nos. 45, 48.

[2] BNFPD, no. 28.

[3] BNFPD, no. 28.

[4] BNFPD, nos. 49-50, italics added. See CIC, c. 236.

[5] CL, no. 9, citing 1 Tm 5:22.

[6] BNFPD, no. 82.

[7] BNFPD, no. 26.

[8] BNFPD, no. 16.

[9] BNFPD, no. 26.

[10] BNFPD, no. 22.

[11] BNFPD, no. 27.

[12] BNFPD, no. 27.

[13] PDO, no. 4.

[14] PDG (1984), no. 94.

[15] PDG (1984), no. 99.

[16] PDG (1984), no. 99.

[17] PDG (1984), no. 75.

[18] PDG (1984), no. 78.

[19] PDG (1984), no. 84.

[20] PDG (1984), no. 84.

[21] PDG (1984), no. 84.

[22] PDG (1984), no. 85.

[23] BNFPD, no. 82.

[24] BNFPD, no. 80.

[25] BNFPD, no. 80.

[26] BNFPD, no. 80.

[27] BNFPD, no. 23.

[28] CL, nos. 7, 8.

[29] The recommendation and vote on each request are to be recorded and attached to the written report submitted to the diocesan bishop. All documentation generated by the committee should be maintained. See CL.

[30] See CL, enclosures II and III; BNFPD, no. 59; CIC, c. 1035 §1.

[31] See CL, enclosures II and III.

[32] CL, enclosure II, no. 1.

[33] CL.

[34] CL, enclosure IV, no. 3.

[35] CIC, c. 1035 §2.

[36] CL, no. 1.

[37] See CIC, c. 1036.

[38] CL, no. 8; CIC, c. 1050 3°.

[39] See CIC, c. 1051 1°.

[40] CL, no. 8; CIC, c. 1051 2°.

[41] CL.

[42] The recommendation and vote on each request are to be recorded and attached to the written report submitted to the diocesan bishop. All documentation generated by the committee should be maintained. See CL.

[43] BNFPD, nos. 57-59.

[44] BNFPD, no. 59.

[45] CIC, c. 1035 §2; BNFPD, no. 59.

[46] CIC, c. 1039; BNFPD, no. 65.

[47] See CIC, c. 833 6°.

[48] "Those in sacred orders invalidly attempt marriage." CIC, c. 1087. See also CIC, c. 1044, §1 3°.

[49] CL.

[50] BNFPD, no. 65.

[51] See CIC, c. 1053 §§1-2.

[52] See CIC, c. 1054.

Chapter Seven

Post-Ordination Stage of Diaconal Formation

I.
Introduction

251.

THE POST-ORDINATION STAGE of diaconal formation "is first and foremost a process of continual conversion."[1]

> [It] requires that ongoing formation strengthen in [each deacon] the consciousness and willingness to live in informed, active and mature communion with their diocesan bishops and priests of their diocese, and with the Supreme Pontiff who is the visible foundation of the entire Church's unity. When formed in this way, they can become in their ministry effective promoters of communion. . . . The continuing formation of deacons is a human necessity which must be seen in continuity with the divine call to serve the Church in the ministry and with the initial formation given to deacons, to the extent that these are considered two initial moments in a single, living, process of Christian and diaconal life.[2]

The goal for this stage of formation is to responsibly address the various aspects of a deacon's ministry, the development of his personality and, above all, his commitment to spiritual growth. "Ongoing formation must include and harmonize all dimensions of the life and ministry of the deacon. Thus . . . it should be complete, systematic and personalized in its diverse aspects whether human, spiritual, intellectual or pastoral."[3] The primary source for post-ordination formation is the ministry itself.

The deacon matures in its exercise and by focusing his own call to holiness on the fulfillment of his social and ecclesial duties, in particular, of his ministerial functions and responsibilities. The formation of deacons should, therefore, concentrate in a special way on awareness of their ministerial character.[4]

252.

The post-ordination stage of formation is motivated by the same dynamism as the holy order received. As St. Paul wrote to Timothy: "Do not neglect the gift you have, which was conferred on you through the prophetic word with the imposition of hands. . . . Be diligent in these matters, be absorbed in them, so that your progress may be evident to everyone. Attend to yourself and to your teaching; persevere in both tasks, for by doing so you will save both yourself and those who listen to you" (1 Tm 4:14-16).

II.
The Dimensions of Formation in the Post-Ordination Stage

253.

The post-ordination stage provides the deacon with ample opportunities to continue to develop and integrate the dimensions of formation into his life and ministry.[5] This ensures the quality of his life and ministry, avoiding the risk of ministerial burnout. In certain cases of difficulty, such as discouragement or a change in ministry, post-ordination formation can entail a process of renewal and revitalization.

254.

In designing the content for an ongoing formation program, those responsible "should take into consideration two distinct but closely related levels of formation: the diocesan level, in reference to the diocesan bishop. . . . and the community level in which the deacon exercises his own ministry, in reference to the parish priest."[6] The deacon is ordained for service to the diocesan Church, even though the focus of that service will usually be within a particular parochial community. Keeping a balance in this dual relationship is essential to his effectiveness as a deacon.

255.

Just as the role of the wife and children were to be carefully discerned throughout the aspirant and candidate stages in formation, this discernment is equally important in the post-ordination stage. It is appropriate to recognize the importance of the ongoing formation of the wives and families of deacons and to provide formation resources and opportunities for them. A family life perspective remains an essential point of reference. Care must, however, be exercised so that "the essential distinction of roles and the clear independence of the ministry" are maintained.[7]

256.

Some deacons, because of a strong desire to function in their diaconal ministries, may dismiss valid areas of concern and conflict with their spouse and family. This dismissal is to be avoided. A married deacon and his family must be instructed on how to request help early when they experience a need. "Unfortunately, our society still focuses almost exclusively on a remedial approach; families [usually] seek help [only] after a crisis has occurred and other problems develop. An alternative is a preventive strategy."[8]

Human Dimension: Developing "Human Qualities As Valuable Instruments for Ministry"[10]

257.

To effectively carry out his diaconal ministry, the deacon must extend himself generously in various forms of human relations without discrimination so that he is perceived by others as a credible witness to the sanctity and preciousness of human life. Post-ordination formation should enable the deacon to pursue this witness to the faith with greater effectiveness. Cultural sensitivity is an important trait for the deacon, as he may be called upon to minister to others who do not share his culture or his native language. It is also important for the pastor who is assigned a deacon to be sensitive in identifying and helping to address any cultural challenges that the deacon may face in this assignment.

Spiritual Dimension: "Diaconal Spirituality"[11]

258.

In Baptism, each disciple receives the universal call to holiness. In the reception of the Sacrament of Holy Orders, the deacon receives a "new consecration to God" through which he is configured to Christ the Servant and sent to serve God's People. Growth into holiness, therefore, is "a duty binding all the faithful." But "for the deacon it has a further basis in the special consecration received. It includes the practice of the Christian virtues and the various evangelical precepts and counsels according to [his] own state of life."[12] The celibate deacon should, therefore, "be especially careful to give witness to [his] brothers and sisters by [his] fidelity to the celibate life the better to move them to seek those values consonant with man's transcendent vocation."[13] He also must be "faithful to the spiritual life and duties of [his] ministry in a spirit of prudence and vigilance, remembering that 'the spirit is willing but the flesh is weak.'"[14] For the married deacon, the Sacrament of Matrimony

> is a gift from God and should be a source of nourishment for [his] spiritual life. . . . it will be necessary to integrate these various elements [i.e., family life and professional responsibilities] in a unitary fashion, especially by means of shared prayer. In marriage, love becomes an interpersonal giving of self, a mutual fidelity, a source of new life, a support in times of joy and sorrow: in short, love becomes service. When lived in faith, this family service is for the rest of the faithful an example of the love of Christ. The married deacon must use it as a stimulus of his diakonia in the Church.[15]

To foster and nurture his diaconal ministry and lifestyle according to his state in life, each deacon must be rooted in a spirit of service that verifies "a genuine personal encounter with Jesus, a trusting dialogue with the Father, and a deep experience of the Spirit."[16]

259.

Some recommended spiritual exercises to assist the deacon in developing and promoting his spiritual life include the following:

a. Daily or frequent participation in the Eucharist, the source and summit of the Christian life[17]
b. Daily or frequent Eucharistic Adoration, as often as his secular employment and family requirements permit
c. It is laudable to develop the habit of monthly celebration of the Sacrament of Penance
d. Daily celebration of the Liturgy of the Hours, at the very least Morning and Evening Prayer[18]
e. Shared prayer with his family
f. Meditative prayer on holy Scripture—*lectio divina*
g. Devotion to Mary, the Mother of God
h. Prayerful preparation of oneself prior to celebrating the sacraments, preaching, or beginning one's ministry of charity
i. Theological reflection
j. Monthly spiritual direction (recommended)
k. Participation in an annual retreat[19]
l. Authentic living of one's state of life
m. Time for personal and familial growth

Intellectual Dimension: Theological Renewal[20]

260.

The intellectual dimension of diaconate formation does not end with ordination but is an ongoing requirement of the vocation. The theological demands of the call to a singular ministry of ecclesial service and pastoral servant-leadership require of deacons a growing love for the Church—for God's holy People—shown by their faithful and competent carrying out of their proper functions and responsibilities. The intellectual dimension of post-ordination formation must be systematic and substantive, deepening the intellectual content initially studied during the candidate stage of formation. Study days, renewal courses, and participation in academic institutes are appropriate formats to achieve this goal. In particular,

> Ongoing formation cannot be confined simply to updating; it should seek to facilitate a practical configuration of the deacon's entire life to Christ who loves all and serves all. . . . In addition, it is

of the greatest use and relevance to study, appropriate and diffuse the social doctrine of the Church. A good knowledge of that teaching will permit many deacons to mediate it in their different professions, at work and in their families. [It may also be useful to] the diocesan bishop [to] invite those who are capable to specialize in a theological discipline and obtain the necessary academic qualifications at those pontifical academies or institutes recognized by the Apostolic See which guarantee doctrinally correct information.[21]

Pastoral Dimension: "Pastoral Methodology for an Effective Ministry"[22]

261.

Pastoral formation constantly encourages the deacon "to perfect the effectiveness of his ministry of making the love and service of Christ present in the Church and in society without distinction, especially to the poor and to those most in need. Indeed, it is from the pastoral love of Christ that the ministry of deacons draws its model and inspiration."[23] When the diaconate is conceived from the start as an integral part of an overall pastoral plan, deacons will have a richer and firmer sense of their own identity and purpose. Thus, an ongoing pastoral formation program responds to the concerns and issues pertinent to the deacon's life and ministry, in keeping with the pastoral plan of the diocesan Church and in loyal and firm communion with the Supreme Pontiff and with his own diocesan bishop.

III.
Additional Considerations

Specialization Programming

262.

"The ministry of the word leads to ministry at the altar, which in turn prompts the transformation of life by the liturgy, resulting in charity."[24] As a deacon eventually focuses on more specific ministries through his responsiveness to the growing needs of the people he serves, it will be necessary to provide more specific programming designed to address his personal needs, talents, and ministry. Initially, however, consideration should be given to deepening his understanding and skills in the ministries of the word, liturgy, and charity.

Program for the Newly Ordained: First Five Years of Diaconate Ministry

263.

There are particular matters relevant to the newly ordained. It is important, therefore, that the newly ordained begin their ministry in a positive and supportive manner. A program is to be planned for the first five years of their ministry and coordinated by the Director of the Permanent Diaconate. In the early phase of their ministry, ongoing formation will largely reinforce the basic training and its application in ministerial practice. Later formation will entail a more in-depth study of the various components proposed in the dimensions in diaconal formation. Consideration also should be given to the newly ordained deacon's conversational study of a second language used within the diocese and the study of its cultural environment. Deacons, as ministers of Christ the Servant, should be prepared to link people of diverse languages and cultures into the local faith community of the diocese and parish. Deacons in their initial pastoral assignments should be carefully supervised by an exemplary designated pastor or priest supervisor especially appointed to this task by the diocesan bishop.[25]

Program for the Newly Widowed Deacon

264.

Those deacons who are recently widowed face unique challenges in their new life situation. In addition to providing support through the grieving process, the diocesan bishop should, at an appropriate time, ensure the deacon is provided with formation to help him understand the implications of the lifelong celibate state that is now his own.[26] The widowed deacon will also benefit from resources for healthy celibate living, such as spiritual reading on celibacy, a support group with other celibate clerics, additional spiritual direction, and counseling. Such formation will include leading the deacon into deeper contemplative prayer, so that he may better embrace the solitude that comes with the loss of his wife. His promise of celibacy that may have remained theoretical has become real. The widowed deacon is now invited into a consecrated love of Christ in celibate chastity. He may become more available to the needs of the Church, which has implications for a deacon's personal life and ministry. The diocesan bishop should discern with the widowed deacon if he can accept more substantive ministerial and spiritual responsibilities.

New Evangelization: The Deacon in the Third Christian Millennium

265.

"The vocation of the permanent deacon is a great gift of God to the Church and for this reason is 'an important enrichment for the Church's mission.'"[27] Being called and being sent by the Lord have always been important, but in contemporary historical circumstances they acquire a particular urgency. "The mission of Christ the Redeemer, which is entrusted to the Church, is still very far from completion. . . . An overall view of the human race shows that this mission is still only beginning and that we must commit ourselves wholeheartedly to its service."[28] To this end, the ministry of the deacon holds great promise, especially for the urgent missionary and pastoral work of the new evangelization. The post-ordination stage of diaconal formation should give priority to this task. Pope Francis exhorts, "All of us are asked to obey his call to go forth from our own comfort zone in order to reach all the 'peripheries' in need of the light of the Gospel."[29]

IV. Diocesan Organization for Post-Ordination Stage Formation

A Diocesan Post-Ordination Program

266.

With the approval of the diocesan bishop, a program for the ongoing formation of deacons should be designed annually. It must take into consideration the demands made upon the deacons by their pastoral ministry, distances to be traveled, the frequency of gatherings, their time commitments to their families and secular employment, and the differing ages and needs of the deacons. In some places, regional or interdiocesan collaboration should be given serious consideration.[30] The use of distance-learning modules also should be explored, especially when travel is a hardship.[31]

Diocesan Policy

267.

Each diocesan Church is to establish a basic minimum of continuing education hours to be fulfilled on an annual basis by all diocesan deacons in active service.[32] This would be in addition to time allocated for the annual diaconal community retreat.[33]

Models for Post-Ordination Formation

268.

At times, the post-ordination stage of diaconal formation may be accomplished in common with priests, religious, and laity of the diocese to enhance collaborative ministerial formation in the diocese. This would use the resources of the diocese in a prudent manner.[34] However, sensitivity to the timing of such events is important, especially for deacons who are engaged in secular employment. On other occasions, ongoing formation programs should be specifically designed for deacons and particularly address the threefold ministry of word, liturgy, and charity.

269.

The models presented earlier in aspirant and candidate formation all lend themselves to a post-ordination formation methodology. Some additional possibilities might include the following:

a. Diocesan, regional, or national conferences
b. Workshops and seminars

c. Educational and developmental themes for retreats and days of recollection
d. Self-guided study
e. Distance learning
f. Ministry reflection groups
g. Mentoring groups among deacons that meet to discuss ministry, exchange experiences, advance formation, and encourage each other in fidelity

Norms

1. A program is to be planned for the first five years of ministry. A newly ordained deacon should be supervised by a designated pastor or supervisor appointed to this ministry by the diocesan bishop. The program should be coordinated by the Director of the Permanent Diaconate. (263)
2. Each diocesan Church should establish a basic minimum of continuing education hours to be fulfilled on an annual basis by all diocesan deacons in active service. (267)

---

[1] DMLPD, no. 65.

[2] DMLPD, nos. 71, 63.

[3] DMLPD, no. 68; see no. 68 note 204.

[4] DMLPD, no. 75.

[5] DMLPD, no. 68.

[6] DMLPD, no. 76.

[7] DMLPD, no. 81.

[8] FP, 33.

[9] DMLPD, no. 69.

[10] DMLPD, no. 70.

[11] DMLPD, no. 44, citing Second Vatican Council, *Decree on the Ministry and Life of Priests* (*Presbyterorum Ordinis*) (December 7, 1965), no. 12a.

[12] DMLPD, no. 45.

[13] DMLPD, no. 60.

[14] DMLPD, no. 60; Mt 26:41.

[15] DMLPD, no. 61.

[16] PDV, no. 72.

[17] These recommendations presuppose that he is already meeting his obligations to attend Sunday Mass and all Holy Days of Obligation. See CIC, c. 1247.

[18] See this *National Directory*, no. 95; CIC, c. 276 §2 3°; and complementary legislation from the United States Conference of Catholic Bishops, "Canon 276, §2, 3°—Permanent Deacons and the Liturgy of the Hours," *www.usccb.org/beliefs-and-teachings/what-we-believe/canon-law/complementary-norms/canon-276-2-3-priests-and-deacons-and-the-liturgy-of-the-hours*.

[19] See CIC, c. 276 §2 4°.

[20] DMLPD, no. 72. See also nos. 65, 71.

[21] DMLPD, nos. 67, 72.

[22] DMLPD, no. 73.

[23] DMLPD, no. 73. In addition, "for adequate pastoral formation it is necessary to hold encounters whose main objective is reflection of the pastoral plan of the Diocese." Congregation for the Clergy, *Directory for the Ministry and the Life of Priests*, new ed. (Vatican City: Libreria Editrice Vaticana, 2013), no. 96. (This is analogous for diaconal formation.)

[24] DMLPD, no. 39.

[25] DMLPD, no. 77.

[26] See this *National Directory*, nos. 79, 80, and 225.

[27] PDO, no. 2.

[28] RM, no. 1.

[29] EG, no. 20.

[30] DMLPD, no. 79.

[31] See this *National Directory*, chapter eight, nos. 277-278, on distance learning.

[32] DMLPD, no. 76.

[33] See this *National Directory*, no. 105, regarding funding.

[34] DMLPD, no. 78.

Chapter Eight

Organization, Structure, and Personnel for Diaconal Formation

I.
Organization

Diocesan Plan for Diaconal Ministry

270.

THE REESTABLISHMENT OR RENEWAL of diaconal ministry within a diocesan Church is best conceived and established within an overall diocesan plan for ministry in which the diaconate is seen as an integral component in addressing pastoral needs. In this way, deacons, who are ordained for service to the diocesan Church, will have a richer and firmer sense of their identity and purpose, as will those who collaborate in ministry with them.

Resources for Organization

271.

Primary resources to guide a diocese in its discernment and readiness for the reestablishment or renewal of the diaconate are the *Code of Canon Law* and other documents of the Holy See, such as the *Basic Norms for the Formation of Permanent Deacons* and *Directory for the Ministry and Life of Permanent Deacons*, in addition to this *National Directory for the Formation, Ministry, and Life of Permanent Deacons in the United States*. These resources establish norms and directives that each diocese is to follow in the formation, ministry, and life of their deacons. Those responsible for the planning and implementation of the diaconal program should be thoroughly familiar with the intent and content of these documents.

272.

The Secretariat for Clergy, Consecrated Life, and Vocations of the United States Conference of Catholic Bishops is also at the service of the diocesan bishop, especially regarding procedures for planning, requesting review of a formation proposal, and implementing the diaconate. Formal review of existing programs by a visiting team organized by the Bishops' Committee on Clergy, Consecrated Life, and Vocations is another resource available through the secretariat.

II.
Structures

Diocesan Program for Diaconal Formation

273.

"The diocese should provide appropriate structures for the formation,"[1] ministry, and life of deacons. Structures include an office, a policy board, a commission on admissions, and so on. Some practical functions of a diocesan diaconate formation structure include collaboration, formation planning, policy development, and post-ordination activities.[2]

Models for Diaconal Formation

274.

Various models for diaconal formation have developed in the United States of America. They provide the essential components for diaconal formation independently or in affiliation with other institutions.

1. The **freestanding** structure is the most common model for diaconal formation in the United States of America. Within this diocesan structure, diaconal formation takes place in its entirety, usually with personnel drawn from the various academic, spiritual, and formational resources of the diocese.
2. The **college/university**-related model incorporates one or more parts of formation from diocesan staff and resources, while one or several parts of formation, such as the intellectual and/or pastoral,

are provided and supervised by a Catholic college or university, usually located within the diocese. In these situations, diocesan coordinators carefully and comprehensively integrate the components of formation. Similar to the college/university model is the model that involves **a graduate school of theology**.

3. A **diocesan or religious seminary** may offer valuable resources for the formation of deacons. The unique and dedicated role of the seminary for priestly formation and the distinction between priestly and diaconal identities must be maintained. "Prudent, limited" use of seminary facilities may be a useful resource available to the diocesan bishop in the formation of participants in a diaconal formation program.[3]
4. In a **collaborative** model, several specific groups, such as religious institutes or dioceses of a province, may choose to unite their resources. The groups maintain separate formation directors and selection processes, but they join together for one or more parts of formation. Care must be taken to ensure that the various components of formation are integrated in a comprehensive manner so that each participating group has a clear understanding of its specific responsibilities.

Distance Learning

275.

Regional provinces, as well as large individual dioceses, may consider employing distance learning as an alternative model for achieving part of the intellectual and pastoral dimensions of diaconal formation. The flexibility that distance learning offers can be a desirable feature in diaconal formation, because it honors a family life perspective in formation and ministry and recognizes the multiple demands on the participants that can make it difficult to be present at one location.[4]

276.

In the United States of America, a significant number of educational institutions, such as local community colleges or universities, have the capacity to conduct video interactive conferencing with multiple sites.

This technology provides one format for distance learning and is usually available to organizations and institutions as a public service. Some dioceses in the United States of America make good use of this technology.

277.

Another rapidly developing distance-learning format is the online seminar. Through the accessibility of the Internet, online seminars and courses in theological, pastoral, and religious studies are being expanded and offer quality programming at a reasonable cost to the participant. These courses are offered at undergraduate, graduate, and adult extension levels through Catholic colleges and universities in the United States of America and throughout the world. If a distance-learning format is incorporated into the diocesan program for part of the intellectual and pastoral dimensions in formation, it is the responsibility of the diocesan bishop to verify that the course of study offered fulfills the requirements of the *Basic Norms for the Formation of Permanent Deacons*, the *Directory for the Ministry and Life of Permanent Deacons*, and this *National Directory*. The course must be complete, be in harmony with magisterial teaching, and be taught by a competent instructor. Of particular interest in distance learning is the availability on the Internet of major theological libraries and research centers throughout the world. A valuable resource in this regard is the website of the Congregation for the Clergy, *www.clerus.org*.[5]

278.

Although coming together as a diaconal formation community is essential, distance learning can be a powerful instrument that supports a family perspective in diaconal formation, as well as an adult's capacity for self-formation with professional guidance.

III.
The Role of the Diocesan Bishop in Diaconate Formation

279.

In the formation of deacons, "the first *sign and instrument* of the Spirit of Christ is the proper Bishop. . . . He is the one ultimately responsible for the discernment and formation" of aspirants and candidates, as well as the pastoral care of deacons.[6] He discharges this responsibility personally, as well as through "suitable associates" who assist him—including the Director of the Permanent Diaconate. The Director is accountable directly to the diocesan bishop or, in his absence, to a cleric whom the diocesan bishop has appointed as his delegate: e.g., vicar general, vicar for the clergy.[7] While the diocesan bishop may exercise his responsibility through his formation associates, nevertheless "he will commit himself, as far as is possible, to knowing personally those who are preparing for the diaconate."[8]

IV.
Recruitment and Preparation of Formation Personnel

280.

Because of the specialized nature of deacon formation, and in order to ensure continuity among program personnel, the diocesan bishop or religious ordinary should encourage experienced and qualified priests and deacons to consider preparing themselves for the apostolate of deacon formation. Religious and lay persons may assist in suitable capacities in deacon formation; those selected by the diocesan bishop to do so should receive appropriate preparation for their role.

Continuity

281.

Continuity in staffing and programming, as well as a planned transition in personnel, ought to receive the highest priority. The administrative staff and formation faculty must comply with the personnel policies established by the diocesan Church for its clergy and lay staff, policies that may include term limits. Such compliance will help in planning for an orderly transition among formation personnel.

282.

Opportunities for sabbaticals, training, and internships for priests, deacons, and professional lay employees in preparation for eventual placements on the diaconal formation staff should be anticipated and scheduled as far in advance as possible.

V.
Aspirant and Candidate Formation Personnel

283.

For the administration of the aspirant and candidate stages in diaconate formation, the following personnel have a special responsibility.

Director of Formation

284.

The director of formation, who must be a priest or a deacon,[9] is appointed by the diocesan bishop to be head of the deacon formation program. He reports directly to the Director of the Permanent Diaconate and should have regular communication with him. The director of formation exercises delegated responsibility for both aspirant and candidate formation. However, the number of participants in either stage may require the additional appointment of an associate. The director of formation oversees the implementation of the formation program. He conducts regularly scheduled assessments; makes home and parish visitations; supervises the formation team, faculty, and mentors; and maintains contact with the aspirants' and candidates' pastors.

285.

The director must be familiar with the diaconate—its history, theology, and practice. He should have parish experience, as well as practical skills and experience in formation, curriculum development, adult educational methodology, vocational discernment, supervision, and administration. He must be capable of providing spiritual leadership to the formation community. In most dioceses, the director of formation fulfills several administrative functions, except the spiritual direction of aspirants and candidates.[10]

Director of Spiritual Formation[11]

286.

The director of spiritual formation assists the director of formation by coordinating the entire spiritual formation program, giving it unity and direction. He provides for the individual spiritual direction of each aspirant and candidate. He also may serve as a spiritual director for an aspirant and/or candidate. He provides an orientation to the spiritual dimension in aspirant and candidate formation to other spiritual directors, who have been chosen by the aspirants or candidates with the approval of the diocesan bishop.[12] The director of spiritual formation provides for the liturgical life and prayer of the aspirant and candidate communities, making appropriate provision for the celebration of the Eucharist, the Liturgy of the Hours, and opportunities to celebrate the Sacrament of Penance in formation gatherings. He is also responsible for retreats and days of recollection, ensuring that they are well planned and carefully executed. The director of spiritual formation, who must be a priest,[13] is nominated by the director of formation and is approved and appointed by the diocesan bishop.

287.

The director of spiritual formation must be dedicated to the Church's *diakonia* and particularly knowledgeable of the diaconate and its mission within the Church. He should possess formal training in spirituality and related areas, including ascetical and mystical theology, pastoral counseling, and referral skills.

Coordinator of Pastoral Formation

288.

An integral formation must relate the human, spiritual, and intellectual dimensions to pastoral practice. "The whole formation imparted [to aspirants and candidates for the diaconate] . . . aims at preparing them to enter into communion with the charity of Christ. . . . Hence their formation in its different aspects must have a fundamentally pastoral character."[14] To ensure that all pastoral formation experiences are closely integrated with the human, spiritual, and intellectual dimensions of formation, the coordinator of pastoral formation assists the director of formation in the apostolic formation of aspirants and candidates. He systematically introduces the aspirants and candidates into suitable pastoral experiences, equipping them with practical skills for pastoral and, eventually, diaconal ministry. The coordinator of pastoral formation, who must be either a priest or a deacon, is nominated by the director of formation and is approved and appointed by the diocesan bishop. The coordinator of pastoral formation corresponds to the office of the "pastor (or other minister)" required by the *Basic Norms for the Formation of Permanent Deacons* of the Congregation for Catholic Education. He administers and coordinates the program of pastoral formation for the aspirant and candidate stages of formation. In consultation with the director of formation and others responsible for formation, he arranges for the pastoral placement of each participant, including an orientation and training of those who assist him in the assignment. Supervisory skills cannot be presumed; teaching them is a high priority. Good supervision guarantees that the pastoral assignment remains systematically educative and formational. The coordinator of pastoral formation also provides a written assessment of the participant's pastoral assignment. The coordinator of pastoral formation has faculty status, thereby ensuring that all pastoral assignments are carefully coordinated with the other dimensions of formation.

289.

It is important that the coordinator of pastoral formation have parish experience, be familiar with pastoral formation, be knowledgeable in theology and supervisory techniques, and be familiar with the value and practice of theological reflection—its goals, objectives, and methods. He should possess formal training in supervision and counseling. Because the pastoral service of the diocesan Church extends to all individuals and groups, including all social classes, with special concern for the poor and those alienated from society, the coordinator of pastoral formation also should have knowledge of the needs and resources within the diocesan Church. He should be familiar with deacon placements within the diocese and their effectiveness in the local Church as well as with ethnic or national or language populations within the diocese.

Professors

Selection

290.

Professors are nominated by the director of formation and are approved and appointed by the diocesan bishop in the freestanding structure, college/university-related model, and diocesan or religious seminary model. In the collaborative model, responsibility belongs to those who hold ecclesiastical jurisdiction; other diocesan bishops who participate should be accorded a voice in the governance of the formation program. The professors contribute in a significant way to the formation of future deacons. The Congregation for Catholic Education has formulated, in its *Directives Concerning the Preparation of Seminary Educators*, specific criteria to guide the selection of professors; these criteria apply to the selection of diaconal professors as well.[15] The criteria established by the Congregation are highlighted in the notes of this chapter.[16] Upon appointment by the diocesan bishop, professors who are charged with teaching philosophical or theological studies must make the Profession of Faith and Oath of Fidelity.[17] Professors must have an appropriate understanding of, and respect for, the proper levels of confidentiality to be observed in formation in the external forum and, if serving as a spiritual director, in the internal forum.

Expectations

291.

Each professor is expected to do the following:

a. Submit a course outline and list of required textbooks.
b. Participate in the assessment of aspirants or candidates for their continuance in the formation process and eventual readiness for ordination to the diaconate.
c. Be available for student consultation, providing feedback to them

on their achievements as well as further development needed.

d. Submit a written assessment of the student's level of achievement in the course, as well as any area that may require further growth.
e. Participate whenever possible in the formation community's life and prayer, discussions, and in-service programming.
f. Be familiar with and experienced in adult learning processes and a family perspective in class preparation, presentation, and assignment.

292.

Professors should expect assistance from the director of formation in the following areas:

a. An **orientation** to the following:
    i. The dimensions in diaconal formation: the formation process, including philosophy, mission, formation goals, and doctrinal understanding of the identity and mission of deacons
    ii. The personal, ministerial, and academic background of current aspirants, candidates, and deacons
b. **In-service programming** that includes the following:
    i. Vatican documents on deacon formation, such as *Basic Norms for the Formation of Permanent Deacons* and *Directory for the Ministry and Life of Permanent Deacons*; the *Instruction on Certain Questions Regarding the Collaboration of the Non-Ordained Faithful in the Sacred Ministry of Priest*
    ii. The *National Directory for the Formation, Ministry, and Life of Permanent Deacons in the United States*
    iii. The role of pastoral assignments in the academic curriculum and assessment
c. **Equitable compensation/stipend** based on travel to and from the formation site, course preparation and grading, and participation in evaluation sessions and meetings, student conferences, and in-service programming—the basic criteria in determining a just stipend are the level of a professor's academic credentials and experience, together with the time commitment in preparing, teaching, and counseling participants
d. An **educational environment** that includes proper equipment, classroom space, and materials

e. **Evaluative comments** from the administrators and students regarding the professor's presentations and response
f. A **formal service agreement** between the director of formation and the individual professor that incorporates the above expectations and that makes as explicit as possible mutual services and obligations

Mentors

293.

The director of formation, with the approval and appointment of the diocesan bishop, should designate mentors from among deacons or priests who are knowledgeable and competent to assist him in assessing the potential and qualifications of those in formation. The mentor is equivalent to the "tutor" described in the *Basic Norms for the Formation of Permanent Deacons*, paragraph 22. The mentor is charged with following the formation of those committed to his care, offering support and encouragement. Depending upon the size of the formation community, a mentor will be responsible for one aspirant or candidate, or he may be invited to minister to a small group of aspirants or candidates. Mentors receive their orientation and supervision from the director of formation. They also help the director for pastoral formation to facilitate theological reflection among those aspirants or candidates assigned to them. Mentors are members of the formation team and are invited "to collaborate with the director of formation in the programming of the different formational activities and in the preparation of the judgment of suitability."[18]

VI.
Advisory Structures for Aspirant and Candidate Stages of Formation

294.

Members of advisory structures should be representative of the pastors, deacons, deacons' wives, religious, and laity. Whenever possible they ought to reflect the variety of cultures and diverse ethnic and racial groups in the diocese. Members may be nominated by the director of formation and be approved and appointed by the diocesan bishop. The director of formation serves as an *ex officio*, non-voting member of any advisory structure.

295.

Advisory structures for the aspirant and candidate stages of formation include the formation policy board and the committee on admission, discussed below.

Formation Policy Board

296.

The diocesan bishop may constitute a formation policy board to assist him and the director of formation in matters of formation. The function of this board is to advise on the planning, implementation, and evaluation of the formation program. Practical skills and experience in curriculum development, formation work, discernment and supervision, spiritual direction, counseling, finances, planning, and organizational development are some of the essential criteria in selecting appropriate board members. The board might also be set up in such a way that not all the members' specific terms of service conclude together, allowing for continuity in the board's deliberations. The membership and procedures of the board should be determined in accordance with its statutes, as approved by the diocesan bishop.

Committee on Admission

297.

The diocesan bishop is to establish a committee on admission, unless another such structure exists. The formation policy board might include this responsibility among its tasks. The committee on admission could, therefore, be constituted as a subcommittee of the formation policy board with its members selected from the board. The specific responsibilities of this committee are to review and recommend applicants for admission to aspirant and candidate formation, nominate aspirants for the Rite of Admission to Candidacy, and review and nominate candidates for institution into the ministries of lector and acolyte and, eventually, for ordination to the diaconate.[19]

VII.
Post-Ordination Formation Personnel

298.

It is a particular responsibility of the diocesan bishop to provide for the pastoral care of the deacons and the diaconal community in his diocese. This care is discharged both personally and through the Director of the Permanent Diaconate. Special care should always be shown to those deacons experiencing difficulties because of personal circumstances. Whenever possible the diocesan bishop should attend the deacons' community meetings, as well as those of the deacon community board or the deacon assignment board, if these structures have been authorized and constituted. If the diocesan bishop is unable to attend, he may designate a cleric—e.g., his vicar general or vicar for the clergy—to represent him in his absence.[20]

Director of the Permanent Diaconate

299.

The diocesan bishop appoints the Director of the Permanent Diaconate. He is directly responsible to the diocesan bishop. The Director, who is to be either a priest or a deacon, should have regular and comprehensive communications with the diocesan bishop on matters regarding individual deacons, as well as their families.[21] In fulfilling his responsibilities, the Director of the Permanent Diaconate must be thoroughly familiar with the intent and context of the Congregation for the Clergy's *Directory for the Ministry and Life of Permanent Deacons* and of this *National Directory*, especially the post-ordination components.

300.

The director serves as the diocesan bishop's representative in implementing the post-ordination stage of diaconate formation. He assists the diocesan bishop in his supervision of the spiritual and personal welfare of deacons and their families. The Director of the Permanent Diaconate supervises the director of formation, who is responsible for those in aspirant and candidate formation. The Director is not, however, personally responsible for those in aspirant and candidate formation.[22]

301.

In most dioceses, the Director of the Permanent Diaconate fulfills several administrative functions, except that of the spiritual direction of deacons.[23] The Director of the Permanent Diaconate, together with the deacon's designated pastor or priest supervisor (if the deacon is assigned to an office or agency not directed by a priest), as well as a representative of that office or agency, and the deacon himself are to be involved in preparing the text of the diocesan bishop's letter of appointment. Further, the director oversees the program for the newly ordained. He also ministers, as delegated by the diocesan bishop, to the other deacons in their assigned ministries, conducting regularly scheduled visits with the deacons and their families, reviewing and evaluating diaconal assignments, and making appropriate recommendations to the diocesan bishop. He assists the diocesan bishop and the deacons' designated pastors in planning and implementing an annual program for diaconate continuing formation. He further assists the diocesan bishop and the designated pastors in their pastoral care of deacons and their families, especially monitoring those living and ministering outside the diocese, or deacons who may be ill or on a ministerial leave of absence. The Director of the Permanent Diaconate also complements the diocesan bishop's presence to and care for retired deacons and their families, as well as to deacon widowers and to widows and their families.

302.

At the discretion of the diocesan bishop, the Director of the Permanent Diaconate may be appointed as a liaison to diocesan departments and public agencies, as well as parishes, on diaconal matters.

VIII.
Post-Ordination Advisory Structures

Deacon Community Board

303.

The diocesan bishop may constitute a deacon community board to represent the deacons and their spouses. Members of such a board would include a suitable number of deacons and wives elected by the diaconal community and others appointed by the diocesan bishop, in accordance with the board's statutes, as approved by the diocesan bishop. The statutes should govern everything that relates to the purposes and operation of the board. A responsibility of the community board could be the preparation of a deacon personnel handbook, specifying appropriate norms or policies—rights, obligations, and responsibilities—for deacons serving the diocesan Church. The diocesan bishop must approve this text and promulgate any appropriate norms or policies. This board also could assist the diocesan bishop and Director of the Permanent Diaconate in planning, coordinating, and evaluating the post-ordination educational and spiritual formation program. The diocesan bishop or a cleric designated as the diocesan bishop's delegate in his absence serves as the board's president.[24]

Deacon Assignment Board

304.

It may be desirable for the diocesan bishop to establish a deacon assignment board to assist him in assigning and evaluating deacons. Its role would be analogous to that of the priests' personnel board, which assists the diocesan bishop in ascertaining appropriate and suitable assignments based on the needs of the particular Church and the capabilities of the individual. The establishment of the deacon assignment board could offer a valuable resource to the diocesan bishop and Director of the Permanent Diaconate. If constituted, the diocesan bishop or, in his absence, a cleric designated by the diocesan bishop (e.g., his vicar general, vicar for the clergy) chairs this board. This board should maintain appropriate links to other diocesan entities to ensure a collaborative and integrative approach to the understanding and use of deacons and diaconal ministry throughout the diocese.

Norms

1. The diocesan bishop is the one ultimately responsible for the discernment and formation of aspirants and candidates, as well as the pastoral care of deacons. He exercises his responsibility personally, as well as through the Director of the Permanent Diaconate, whom he has appointed. The Director of the Permanent Diaconate, who must always be a cleric, is responsible directly to the diocesan bishop or, in his absence, to a cleric whom the bishop has appointed as his delegate. (279)
2. The director of formation, who must be either a priest or a deacon, is appointed by the diocesan bishop to be head of the deacon formation program. He is directly responsible to the Director of the Permanent Diaconate. (284)
3. The diocesan bishop may set up a formation policy board to assist him and the director of formation in matters of diaconal formation. (296)
4. The director of spiritual formation, who must be a priest, is nominated by the director of formation. He is approved and appointed by the diocesan bishop. He personally oversees the spiritual formation of each participant and provides an orientation to other spiritual directors, who must also be priests and who may be chosen by the aspirants or candidates with the approval of the diocesan bishop. (286, 287)
5. The coordinator of pastoral formation, who corresponds to "the pastor (or other minister)" required by the *Basic Norms for the Formation of Permanent Deacons* of the Congregation for Catholic Education, is nominated by the director of formation. He is a cleric who is approved and appointed by the diocesan bishop. (288, 289)
6. Professors are nominated by the director of formation and then are approved and appointed by the diocesan bishop. (290)
7. Mentors for aspirants and candidates, who are to be knowledgeable and competent to assist the director of formation, are nominated

from among priests and deacons by the director of formation. They also are approved and appointed by the diocesan bishop. Mentors are charged with closely following the formation of those committed to their care, offering support and encouragement. (293)

8. If a distance-learning model is incorporated into the diocesan formation program, it is the responsibility of the diocesan bishop to verify that the course of study offered fulfills the requirements of this *Directory*. It must be complete, be in harmony with magisterial teaching, and be taught by a competent instructor. (275-278)
9. The diocesan bishop should appoint a Director of the Permanent Diaconate, who should be either a priest or a deacon. At the discretion of the diocesan bishop, the Director of the Permanent Diaconate serves as the diocesan bishop's representative in directing the post-ordination stage of formation and assists the diocesan bishop in supervising diocesan deacons. This director also coordinates the program for the newly ordained deacons. (43, 299-302)

---

[1] PDG (1984), no. 52.

[2] Some of the specific responsibilities would include the following:

Collaboration

i. Involvement of and accountability to the diocesan bishop
ii. Relationship with diocesan offices, departments, and agencies; linkage with other ministry preparation programs in the diocese
iii. Liaison with pastors, priests, religious, and laity
iv. Relationship with regional and national diaconate associations and organizations

Planning

i. Appointment, readiness, and supervision of appropriate personnel to carry out the diaconal formation plan/activities
ii. Initial and ongoing catechesis of the diaconate
iii. Integrate diaconal ministry into the local Church

Policy Development

i. Development of policies and procedures for recruitment, screening, and admissions
ii. Development of policies and procedures for evaluation of those in formation
iii. Development of the program, taking account of concrete needs and local circumstances

Post-Ordination Activities

i. Development of policies and procedures for diocesan diaconal life
ii. Support structures for deacons, deacon spouses, and families
iii. Policies/procedures for assignment and review of deacons
iv. Continuing formation and spiritual formation policies and program opportunities
v. Regular assessment of diaconal ministry in the diocese

[3] Congregation for Catholic Education and the Congregation for the Clergy, *Joint Study of the US Draft Document–The National Directory for the Formation, Ministry and Life of Permanent Deacons in the United States*, Prot. No. 78/2000 (March 4, 2002).

[4] See GDC, no. 160.

[5] The Congregation for the Clergy offers its website to assist in the continuing formation of priests and deacons. The website provides a library on the magisterial teachings of the Roman pontiffs, with recent documentation from the Holy Father, Church Fathers, and sacred writings. It provides links to several theological libraries; live teleconferences or documentation from the teleconferences on Christology, ecclesiology, sacramental and moral theology, Mariology, pneumatology; statistical information on diocesan and religious priests and deacons; as well as an email option for updated information on future offerings.

[6] BNFPD, no. 19.

[7] BNFPD, no. 16. See also nos. 21, 42, 44, 62; DMLPD, nos. 3, 78, 80.

[8] BNFPD, no. 19.

[9] BNFPD, no. 21.

[10] BNFPD, no. 21.

[11] BNFPD, no. 23.

[12] PDV, no. 57. See BNFPD, no. 85.

[13] "It is the intention of our Dicasteries that the variety of offices in diaconal formation and post-ordination ministry: the Director of the Formation Program, the Coordinator for Pastoral Formation, Mentors, the Director of the Permanent Diaconate should be reserved to clerics—and in the case of the Director of Spiritual Formation (an office not mentioned in the *Ratio fundamentalis*), Pastors and Priest Pastoral Supervisors, they must be a priest." Congregation for Catholic Education and the Congregation for the Clergy, *Joint Study of the US Draft Document—The National Directory for the Formation, Ministry and Life of Permanent Deacons in the United States*, Prot. No. 78/2000 (March 4, 2002).

[14] PDV, no. 57.

[15] Congregation for Catholic Education, *Directives Concerning the Preparation of Seminary Educators* (Washington, DC: United States Catholic Conference, 1994), 5-6.

[16] The following considerations are this Directory's commentaries on the criteria for faculty selections as established by the Congregation for Catholic Education:

i. *A spirit of faith*: A lived commitment to the Church, its Magisterium, and the Deposit of Faith accompanied and sustained by a love of prayer—the educator who lives by faith teaches more by what he is than by what he says
ii. *A pastoral sense*: A commitment to the pastoral-theological vision of the Second Vatican Council and to the identity and mission of diaconal ministry that the Council and post-conciliar documents promote in the Church; a sensitivity also from their own participation in the pastoral charity of Christ
iii. *A spirit of communion*: Collaboration and understanding of their role in the vocational discernment for admission to candidacy and ordination to the diaconate

iv. *Human maturity and psychological equilibrium*: A right consciousness of oneself, of one's own values and limits, honestly recognized and accepted
v. *A clear and mature capacity to love*: An ability to be an example and model of the primacy of love in service—a capacity and inclination to offer self-giving attention to the other person, to an understanding of his or her concerns, and to a clear perception of his or her real good
vi. *Listening, dialogue, and the capacity for communication*: The success of the formational relationship depends in great part on these three capacities
vii. *Positive and critical attention to modern culture*: Inspired by the cultural richness of Christianity (i.e., rooted in biblical, liturgical, and patristic sources), a broad knowledge of contemporary culture—a positive and critical awareness of the transmission of contemporary culture, making it easier to enable students to form an interior synthesis in the light of faith.

The following are additional criteria:

i. *Academic qualifications*: An advanced degree in theology, religious studies, or a related field; a demonstrated ability as a competent teacher
ii. *Multicultural sensitivity*: Experience with multicultural, gender, economic, and educational diversity
iii. *Adult formation*: Ability to teach adults in theory and practice; knowledge and experience in adult developmental theory and methodologies
iv. *Diversity*: Represent the ethnicity, racial, and cultural diversity of the diocesan Church
v. *Knowledge and experience of the diaconate*: Knowledge of the identity and ministry of deacons in the Church

[17] See CIC, c. 833 6°-7°.

[18] BNFPD, no. 22.

[19] CL.

[20] DMLPD, no. 80.

[21] See BNFPD, no. 21. The phrase "could be either a priest or a deacon" is applied equivalently in this *National Directory* to the position of the director of the permanent diaconate.

[22] BNFPD, no. 21.

[23] BNFPD, no. 21.

[24] DMLPD, no. 80.

[25] BNFPD, no. 24.

Conclusion

305.

IT IS THE DESIRE of the United States Conference of Catholic Bishops that, as implemented in accord with local or regional resources, this *National Directory* will provide a sure directive for promoting harmony and unity in diaconal formation and ministry throughout the dioceses of the USCCB, as well as within the Personal Ordinariate of the Chair of St. Peter. In so doing, this *National Directory* will ensure a certain uniformity in the identity, selection, and formation of deacons, as well as provide for more clearly defined pastoral objectives in diaconal ministries.

306.

This *National Directory* is presented to the diaconal communities in the United States of America as a tangible expression of the USCCB's gratitude to them for their dedicated ministry to God's People. It is also intended to challenge and encourage them to be, with greater dedication and clarity, "a specific sacramental sign, in the Church, of Christ the Servant."[1]

---

[1] BNFPD, no. 5.

Index

Locators in this index generally refer to paragraph numbers. Notes are indicated by the number/name of the chapter, a lowercased "note," and the note number (preface*note*6; ch1note42). Norms are identified by the chapter they follow, and the norm number (ch2norm12).

Scriptural Index

Locators in this index generally refer to paragraph numbers. Notes are indicated by the number/name of the chapter, a lowercased "note," and the note number (preface*note*6; ch1note42). Norms are identified by the chapter they follow, and the norm number (ch2norm12).